S. W. Henley, S. W. Henley

The Cash Family of South Carolina

A Truthful Account of the many Crimes Committed by the Carolina Cavalier

Outlaws

S. W. Henley, S. W. Henley

The Cash Family of South Carolina
A Truthful Account of the many Crimes Committed by the Carolina Cavalier Outlaws

ISBN/EAN: 9783743419285

Manufactured in Europe, USA, Canada, Australia, Japa

Cover: Foto ©ninafisch / pixelio.de

Manufactured and distributed by brebook publishing software (www.brebook.com)

S. W. Henley, S. W. Henley

The Cash Family of South Carolina

THE CASH FAMILY OF SOUTH CAROLINA.

A Truthful Account of the Many Crimes Committed by the Carolina Cavalier Outlaws.

By S. W. HENLEY,
EDITOR WADESBORO INTELLIGENCER.

Price, Fifty Cents.

INTELLIGENCER PRINT,
Wadesboro, Anson County, N. C.
1884.

THE CASH FAMILY

OF

SOUTH CAROLINA.

A TRUTHFUL ACCOUNT OF THE MANY CRIMES COMMITTED BY THE CAROLINA CAVALIER OUTLAWS.

By S. W. HENLEY,

EDITOR WADESBORO INTELLIGENCER.

PRICE FIFTY CENTS.

INTELLIGENCER PRINT:
Wadesboro, Anson County, N. C.
1884.

THE CASH FAMILY OF SOUTH CAROLINA.

By S. W. HENLEY.

"Why, I can smile, and murder while I smile."
[King HENRY VI.

Soft! I did but dream.—
O, coward conscience, how dost thou afflict me!—
The lights burn blue!—It is now dead midnight.
Cold fearful drops stand on my trembling flesh.
What do I fear? myself? there's none else by:
Richard loves Richard; that is, I am I.
Is there a murderer here? No;—yes; I am:
Then fly,—What, from myself? Great reason: why?
Lest I revenge. What! Myself upon myself?
Alack! I love myself. Wherefore? for any good,
That I myself have done unto myself?
Oh! no: alas! I rather hate myself,
For hateful deeds committed by myself.
I am a villain. Yet I lie; I am not.
Fool, of thyself speak well:—Fool, do not flatter.
My conscience hath a thousand several tongues,
And every tongue brings on a several tale,
And every tale condemns me for a villain.
Perjury, foul perjury, in the high'st degree;
Murder, stern murder in dir'st degree:
All several sins, all us'd in each degree,
Throng to the bar, crying all,—Guilty! guilty!
I shall despair.—There is no creature loves me;
And if I die, no soul shall pity me:—
Nay, wherefore should they? since that I myself
Find in myself no pity to myself.
Methought, the souls of all that I had murder'd
Came to my tent; and every one did threat
To-morrow's vengeance on the head of Richard."
[King RICHARD III.

Col. E. B. C. CASH.

CHAPTER I.

The Cheraw Tragedy.

Since the famous Cash-Shannon duel in 1880, in which the stainless Shannon fell a martyr to the odious "Code of Honor," and a victim of the Cash's rapacity, these two men, Col. E. B. C. Cash, and William Boggan Cash, his son, have attained a national notoriety, and everything which has been published concerning them has gained interest in the public mind.

Why this should have been true, why they should have become so conspicuous, why the unmeasured execrations of a nation should have been heaped upon the heads of two of its citizens for the commission of an offence when so many prominent and highly respected gentlemen of their day and generation have been guilty of the same offence, and, though equally culpable, have yet not "lost cast" among their fellows, it is difficult to determine, and must be reckoned, perhaps, as an inexplicable social phenomenon of the period.

Nevertheless, such is a fact, and it is here mentioned incidentally, showing, as it must, a marked influence, which, undoubtedly, has operated against the Cashes, and which has so far inflamed the popular mind that few care to believe of them as other than the most hardened, remorseless criminals.

Whether this judgment be righteous, the reader must decide for himself, as he peruses the narrative of their lives.

Prior to the Cash-Shannon duel, the Cashes had only a local reputation, which was neither very good nor very bad. Only in Chesterfield and the counties adjoining were they known, and in all probability there were many people in this region who had never heard of them.

At one time Col. Cash was well thought of by his fellow-citizens, and even now he has many friends and sympathizers who adhere to him in his adversity, which is an evidence that there is something in the make-up of the man of a meritorious nature. To his poor, needy neighbors he is now, and always has been, a friend and benefactor, but no petty lord in the feudal times ever exacted more abject obedience—more slavish submission—on the part of his dependents, than has at all times characterized Col. Cash in his dealings with those around him. He is imperious in the extreme, and cannot brook opposition from any source. His will must be law, or his impulse is to slay whosoever opposes him. It is this intolerant spirit which, year after year allowed to go uncurbed, at all times swaying him as the tempest says the forest, that made Col. Cash what he is. It is a supercillious spirit, which, denying to every one else the right of an opinion, or the right to act in obedience to one's opinions, that has developed Col. Cash into an unreasonable, uncompromising tyrant. It is this dictatorial, overbearing spirit, which, year after year allowed to run riot, without the making of one effort to bridle it, that has forged and welded fetters around the man's life stronger than life itself. It is this vile spirit which, disdaining the rights of others and arrogating unto self the sole right of exacting homage and obedience, and denying mutual concessions in his intercouse with his fellow man, that has crowded Reason from its Throne, Justice from its Temple, Love from its Sanctuary, and rendered Col. Cash the most pitiable slave of his own beastial passions. It was this spirit which goaded him on to the murder of the gentle Shannon, and it is this spirit which has at last undone him.

Immediately after the duel, the comparatively obscure name of Cash sprang into notoriety, and perhaps no participant in any combat which has occurred in America since the time of Aaron Burr, has been so unreservedly censured—so severely abused—as has been Col. Cash for the part he played in that tragic drama.

With the causes which led to the duel I will hereafter deal, but will here take occasion to state that it was due to the agency of Boggan Cash that his father "met" Col. Shannon.

The demon which slumbered in the younger Cash was then little known. True, he had been a party to two bloodless duels before that time, but still there was nothing in his general bearing which gave promise of the desperate career upon which he was about entering. Doubtless there had long been an internal conflict going on—a conflict between native tendency and the ideas of propriety which had been implanted in his mind by education—but the propensities of the man did not reveal themselves in all of their hideousness until after the tragedy at Dubois' Bridge. It is even possible, but for that unhappy episode, Virtue might have gained the ascendency in his heart, and the pious teachings of his mother might have triumphed over the ungodly influence of his father. But for the part he played in bringing about that sad catastrophe, it ispossible that he might have lived to be an ornament and a blessing to the community in which he resided, and where his prospects at one time were most flattering.

However, his feet were already straying in Error's way, and, since his mother's death, there being no virtuous counselor at home to warn and to guide him, he naturally followed the bent of his inclinations, and these, stimulated by his father's teachings and example, proved stronger than his better impulses.

Rapidly did he sink downward. A malign power impelled him onward—resistlessly onward—ever downward. Step by step did he descend into the depths of infamy, until he dyed his hands in human gore and became a fugitive from justice—an outlaw destined to die at the hands of the officers of the law.

At the time of the duel, Boggan was undoubtedly tending downward gradually, but from that day there was a marked change in his bearing and deportment. He seemed to lose his own self respect, and with it vanished his social instincts and all taste for the society of refined and cultivated people. The scorpion last of a guilty conscience was at work, and it scourged him by day and by night.

Formerly he had been the leading spirit of sociality and the soul of generosity—open-hearted, open-handed. For his friends, nothing that he possessed was too good, and he enjoyed no good thing without some friend to share it with him.

Suddenly he became an old man—bitter, malignant, morbid and morose—ready at any moment, with or without provocation, to strike to the death any one who should cross him.

He sought fellowship with the vicious and reprobate, and so rapidly, steadily did he sink downward that soon the lowest, the meanest, the most depraved elements in the social fabric became his boon companions.

Deep drinking, gambling, horse-racing, cock-fighting, and all manner of debauchery became the engrossing objects of his life, and when these diversions palled upon his tastes, it was his wont to go to Cheraw and "run the town" in strict accordance with the typical Western desperado's ethics.

On such occasions the ordinances were totally disregarded and the authorities set at defiance. Many of the business houses would close up and bar their doors, while the proprietors would seek refuge in some secure retreat. In the confusion ensuing, the police, unimpeded, would flee from the vicinage of the ruffian, leaving him in undisputed possession of the place.

In an enlightened, civilized South Carolina town like Cheraw, where the law is sovereign, and where there are ever enough true men to vindicate the law's majesty, such a state of affairs could not always continue. Sooner or later an end must come. At last patience lost its savor and forbearance ceased to be a virtue. The good people of Cheraw were determined to submit to the Cash outrages no longer.

The violence of the Cashes was well known, and it was confidently believed, as asserted, that to arrest one or both of them would be attended with fatal consequences. Though this were true, yet the people of Cheraw were not deterred by emotions of fear—caitiff fear—in hesitating to enforce the ordinances, but they felt, to do so, they might have to shed human blood—and few of the good, the truly brave, care to do this, so long as there is any other alternative. This, and this alone, is the secret of their long forbearace—their Job-like patience—and for being thus tardy in the execution of the law they should not be censured, but commended.

Aside from this, the Cashes were extensively connected in Cheraw, many of the best people of the place being their "blood kin." Furthermore, there were many others, who, while condemning their course, had yet been linked to them by ties of friendship in the past, when they were held in repute, and the remembrance of the past was sufficient to deter them from taking any active part against the Cashes, however much they may have secretly desired to see them brought in subjection to the law.

Whatever the outside world may think of this, the writer of these lines feels assured, after a thorough investigation of the subject, that to the above mentioned causes may be attributed the immunities which were allowed the Cashes, and that no element of cowardly fear, on the part of the citizens, deterred them from treating the Cashes as they would have treated other violators of the law under similar circumstances.

This may be wrong—it is wrong—but it is human nature, nevertheless, and a phase of human nature, too, not altogether reprehensible.

However, there was one man in Cheraw who held nothing in common with the good people of that place, who held no sympathy with the Cashes, and whom the Cashes, in turn, despised as a being beneath their notice.

This man was one W. H. H. Richards, a native of Massachusetts, who followed Sherman to South Carolina during the late war, who was at the burning of Columbia, and who, after the cessation of hostilities, was stationed with the Federal garrison at Cheraw.

This Richards was a bad man—a very bad man. The genial temperature of South Carolina better agreeing with his indolent disposition than the frigid breath of his native hills, he felt no inclination to quit so pleasant a place, and, after receiving his discharge from the army, he decided to there remain.

He ingratiated himself into the esteem of a Chesterfield lady, and to her was married, May 17, 1866—the bride being a mere girl of fifteen years.

Had he possessed one element of manhood—one trait of nobility—he might have lived happily, for the trusting girl who confided her life to his keeping, did well and faithfully perform her part in the battle of existence, but her devotion and her virtues were powerless long to retain the fidelity of her lecherous lord. Neglect and unkind treatment soon marked his conduct toward her, until, at last, he deserted her.

His next act of infamy was to invade another man's home and pollute its sancity (if there can be such a thing as sancity in the home of a man who cannot defend that home, and who still continues to live under the same roof with the woman who has violated her marriage vows—who would deign to live under the same roof with a faithless wife, conscious of her perfidy—conscious that she was another man's paramour.)

I do not know the name of this abject wretch, nor do I want to know it. I only know that he held Richard in such mortal dread, that, when he would hear the usurper's footsteps approaching the home he had desecrated, he, the lawful husband, would flee tremblingly away to the garret or an outhouse, leaving the fireside he could not defend to the foul possession of one who had contaminated all that he should have held dearer than life and sacred as heaven.

Thus behaved the martyr Richards, who, after leading a thriftless, improvident life for several years, at last entered the liquor business and kept a disreputable grogery until he was forced to suspend.

Then came another season of idleness and vagabondage, when the woman with whom he had been living in unholy relations, repudiated him. He then returned to his wronged and deserted wife, who, in the hope that she might be able to reclaim the father of her children, again received him with joy to her arms.

Nobly, well and heroically, did she labor for her family, and it began to appear that Richards would partially atone for his past conduct, and, in a measure, wipe from his name the foul stain which, by his acts, he had cast upon it.

His poor wife was again happy, for, if there is a joy in this world akin to the joy of heaven, it is when a noble, long-suffering woman, after she has beheld the downfall of the man she loves—after she has beheld him reveling in the dust of degradation—at last detects in him a desire to amend—a resolve to be worthy of her love and the esteem of his fellowmen.

Richards continued to live with his wife happily, as far as the world knows, until his death.

In the fall of 1882 he entered the Cheraw police service. Whatever may have been his vices—whatever may have been his crimes—he at least possessed one virtue—courage. No danger ever appalled him, and he was never known to shrink from the discharge of his duty. It is stated, however—but I vouch not for the truth of the statement—that he was unnecessarily violent in the making of arrests, and that a large number of people from Chesterfield and Marlboro counties, who are in the habit of visiting Cheraw, and whose weakness it is, on such occasions, to get a little intoxicated and a little turbulent, held him in dread and abhorrence, because of his brutality. I know not if this be true. It is vouched for by some denied by others. I believe, however, that there is a grain of truth in the statement. But, be it true or be it false, one thing cannot be denied, viz: That he made it a rule to arrest all violators of the ordinances, and that, whenever he "went for a man" he was sure to bring him. And there was one other notable fact—he could not be intimidated by the Cashes, and in his breast their threats aroused no terror. He expressed himself as ready and willing to arrest them as quick as he would any one else; and there can be little doubt of his having entertained a secret desire for an opportunity to present itself, which would afford him a chance of demonstrating the fact that he was not afraid of the Cashes. He had long been nettled with queries similar to this: "Richards, if you are so much of a man, and so brave, why don't you tackle Bog Cash?" To such questions he would generally make a boasting reply, which, after being many times magnified, would invariably be reported to Boggan, who, in turn, becoming exasperated, would retort boastingly and denounce Richards. Doubtless, much was accredited to each of these men and reported to the other, which neither ever dreamed of.

Thus, an antipathy was engendered between them, which was kept alive by secret foes and mischief makers, in the hope that it would eventually result in the removal of one or both from the community.

At last, the crisis came. On the 16th of February, 1884, Boggan Cash visited Cheraw and got drunk. His proceedings on that occasion were faithfully reported in the Wadesboro Intelligencer of February 23, 1884, and as nothing has since transpired to show wherein that report was incorrect, it is here reproduced. Said the Intelligencer:

"Saturday night last, it will be remembered, was a dark and gloomy time. and in harmony with sombre nature were the younger Cash's spirits, Therefore went he to Cheraw and got drunk—gloriously drunk. Then went he out on the streets, hallooing and bellowing, 'Hurrah for Baggan Cash and the Cashes generally!'

"The Marshal sought the boistrous votary of Bacchus and commanded him to be quiet, declaring no such conduct could be tolerated on the streets of Cheraw. Boggan, at the time had his foot in the stirrup and was in the act of mounting his horse. He turned to Richards and said, with a sneer, 'Who are you?' to which Richards replied, 'I am the town marshal.'

With a low growl of contempt, Boggan responded, 'I beg your pardon.'

"His horse, however—a spirited animal—being rather unruly, Boggan, owing to his intoxicated condition, was unable to mount, and continued to damn the horse, which Richards understood as an overt defiance on the part of Boggan.

"Richards, without further ceremony, essayed to lay hands on Boggan, when the latter turned ferociously upon the Marshal and "made for him," catching him in the collar. At this juncture the marshal rapped Mr. Cash across the head with his club, causing him to stagger like unto a bull yearling when the butcher hitteth him between the horns with an axe."

Cash, however, recovered almost instantly, and, still holding the Marshal by the collar, struck at him several times, but the Marshal, having been well instructed in the art of dodging when a boy, evaded the licks aimed at him and at once began to shower terrific blows down on Cash's right arm, which he threw up to shield his head.

"Richards was a man of marvelous strength, and the first blow he struck Cash would have been sufficient to kill an ordinary man, but as nothing short of an infernal machine or a thunderbolt would be efficacious with a Cash, it only stunned Boggan for a second, and then he was himself again—a maniac with rage.

"He had received, however, a fearful gash over the left temple—the flesh being laid open to the bone—while his right arm and shoulder were bruised black as a nigger by the succeeding blows which the Marshal dealt upon him.

"A terrific struggle ensued, and the Marshal would, it seems, have succeeded in caging his man, but for the fact that, as he walked backwards across the street, pulling the offender after him, he stepped off the end of a bridge and fell. Cash fell on top, and, having thus accidentally gained the advantage over his antagonist, he lost no time in turning that advantage to account. Still holding to the Marshal with his left hand, he beat him with his right fist, and then stamped him in the face until he was almost beyond recognition.

"It is possible that he might have beat the Marshal to death, had he not been pulled off by Mr. Peter S. Terry, who, by that time, had arrived upon the scene.

"Boggan then turned upon Mr. Terry in a savage manner and advanced upon him menacingly, but Mr. T. was too quick for him. Whipping out a small volume of explosives, commonly denominated Smith & Wesson, he serenely leveled the same at Mr. Cash and calmly warned him not to approach another inch, or he would quickly make him an angel, 'with a crown upon his forehead and a harp within his hand.'

"Cash, appreciating the fact that Mr. Terry meant business, and that he would do just what he promised, muttered an oath and withdrew.

"By this time the peaceable, long-forbearing, long-suffering people of Cheraw were thoroughly aroused, and if Boggan Cash had not made himself scarce in those diggings, in all probability he would now be sojourning in that place where it is said there is weeping and wailing and gnashing of teeth — where the fire is not quenched and the worm dieth not.

"Boggan, dripping with blood, went to a saloon in the vicinity to get a drink of liquor, with which to revive his spirits and restore his valor, but when he felt for his money, he discovered it to be gone. It is said that before the fracas, he had a considerable sum on his person, and some have charged that Richards, being a nimble-fingered Yankee, attacked Boggan in the first place with a view of robbery.

"We will take occasion to state, however, that no one believes this tale, and we doubt if Col. Cash, who was the first to make it public, really believes it himself.

"Boggan next went to the Timmons Hotel, where he received all necessary attention. After his wounds were dressed he attempted to return home, but loss of blood and the exercise he had just taken, rendered him too weak to travel and he passed the night at the hotel. In the morning a friend carried him home in a buggy, where he has since remained in peace, reflecting, it may be, over the vanity of human affairs, and especially upon the folly of going to Cheraw and getting drunk."

Thus concluded the Intelligencer's report of the first difficulty between Richards and Boggan Cash.

At the time this occurred, Col. Cash was in Laurins, S. C., visiting his daughter, Mrs. R. C. Watts, where, it was reported at the time, he intended making his home.

Whether Boggan notified his father of what had happened, summoning him to aid or abet him in seeking redress, is not known, and the writer believes such to be untrue, although it is possible.

At any rate, Col. Cash reached Cash's Depot about noon, Saturday, February 23rd, and when he arrived, Boggan was in the act of leaving for Cheraw. A hurried conversation ensued, and Boggan rode off, for the purpose, it is claimed, of having his horses shod, one of which he proposed running against a noted racer of Marlboro county the following week. He rode one horse himself and a negro boy rode the other.

The two animals were left at a blacksmith's shop on the outskirts of the town, while Boggan walked up into the town to transact some business. This was between the hours of 1 and 2 o'clock.

Boggan, in the course of the afternoon, passed and repassed

Richards several times, but neither noticed the other. At least they pretended not to notice each other.

On the night of the 16th, soon after the first difficulty, Boggan expressed himself as ruined—disgraced forever—that, to be beat by such a man as Richards, was a humiliation greater than he could bear. He declared that there could be no redress for him, as he could not seek an "honorable" adjustment of his trouble with a man so far beneath the recognition of a gentleman—that his only recourse would be to go out and shoot him down as he would a dog.

This, however, was not put in the shape of a threat, and it was believed by all, that, as soon as his anger should have time to abate, he would reconcile himself to his deserved chastisement.

Having business in Cheraw several times during the succeeding week, he approached to the suburbs of the town, and sent for the parties with whom he had business, to come to him. On each of these visits, he was armed with his pistols and a Winchester rifle, but made no hostile demonstration and no threat escaped his lips.

On one occasion he was invited by the Mayor to enter the town at his pleasure, promising that no effort would be made to arrest him for his offence on the preceding Saturday night. This he declined, averring that he did not wish to see Richards, as he had no disposition to renew the difficulty with him.

As above stated, however, he did enter the town on Saturday, February 23rd, and frequently passed Richards on the streets.

About 4:30 o'clock he entered a saloon for "refreshments," and while there had the pleasure of hearing the saloon keeper read in the Wadesboro Intelligencer the foregoing report of his difficulty with Richards. He was greatly incensed, but while swearing vengeance on the editor of the Intelligencer, made no threat respecting the Marshal.

A few minutes after he left the saloon he met a messenger whom his father had dispatched to him with a note. Upon perusing the note he manifested something of excitement, but immediately tore it up, muttering with an oath, "All right."

He walked off briskly, as if acting under a new and sudden impulse. At this time, Richards was standing on what is known as Brock's Corner (about the most public place in town) leisurely leaning against a tree. He heard not, or heeded not, the approach of Cash, from whom he evidently felt he had nothing to apprehend.

When he had passed a few feet he suddenly halted, and, turning to Richards, asked if he was looking for him. To this, Richards replied, "Not particularly; but, if I were, I would only be doing my duty."

At this Cash commenced firing a No. 38 Smith & Wesson pistol, but the courageous man who saw himself about to be

W. H. H. RICHARDS,
The Marshal of Cheraw, S. C., shot by Boggan Cash, Feb. 23, 1884.

murdered, evinced no sign of terror. He appreciated the fact that his end was at hand, but he had faced danger too often before, to quail now, and, without a fearful tremor, stood erect while the fatal volley was poured upon him. Whatever may be said to his detriment, let it at least be said to his credit that he met his fate as becomes a brave man—that he cooly, calmly, fearlessly faced his murderous foe, and, though unarmed and powerless to resist, made no effort to escape.

This brave and dauntless man had been a soldier on the "other side," and had three times been promoted for valorous conduct on the field of battle, but I venture the assertion that never, in the course of his checkered life, did he act with greater heroism than on that fatal day, when, in the quiet, lovely town of Cheraw, in the discharge of his duty, he fell at the hands of a cowardly assassin.

Three shots were fired in rapid succession. The first shot missed its mark quite two feet, and, striking Mr. James Coward, a by-stander, in one side, penetrated to within a short distance of the other side, where it was cut out by a surgeon.

The second shot struck the Marshal in the breast, pierced one lung, and embedded itself in about the same place that Guiteau's ball found a lodgment in the body of Garfield. The third ball grazed the Marshal's clothing and buried itself in a tree.

Then came a most disgusting scene—the flight of the murderer—which will be dwelt upon hereafter.

In the meantime, let us endeavor to trace, if we can, the immediate cause of the murder in certain developments which have since come to light.

It is claimed that the note which Boggan received from his father after he left the saloon, was a command to murder Richards. If this be true will never be definitely known, unless Col. Cash confesses, but there is certain evidence in support of the idea which is of a most convincing nature.

In a letter addressed to Mr. John T. Agerton, of Cheraw, under date of February 27th, 1874, Col. Cash says: "If Boggan had not killed Richards, I would have done it on the same day he was shot, and if he had recovered I intended to kill him on sight. * * Of course our enemies will blow, but we ask them no sort of odds."

Add to this the statement of Col. Cash, while a prisoner in the Columbia jail, made to a reporter of the Columbia Register, and it will appear evident that his note to Boggan counseled the killing:

"When I reached home Saturday, Boggan was on his way to Cheraw, and we merely passed a few words of greeting. Not a word was said about the difficulty between him and Richards. After he left me, I was fully informed of the unmerciful beating which Richards had given Boggan. I made up my mind, come what may, I would kill Richards before dark. I had my rifle and pistol, and borrowed a second pistol. Every one at the depot, about twenty-five in all, including a minister, heard me declare my intention to kill Richards, and not one advised me against it. While I was waiting for the train to take me to Cheraw, Boggan came dashing up on Border Ruffian. I was in the back part of Dr. Clayton's store when Boggan rode up and told those on the outside of what he had done. A negro rushed into the store and said to me, 'You need not go to Cheraw; the Captain has already killed Richards.' * * I embraced Boggan, and for the first time since he was an infant kissed him, and told him that I was proud of him; that if he had not killed Richards I intended to do so. Boggan did not know, until then, that I had heard of the terrible beating which Richards had given him."

Admitting that Boggan did not summon his father from Laurins, and that Col. Cash knew nothing of the difficulty until after his arrival at Cash's Depot, does it not appear evident from the above, that, as soon as he heard of it, he at once commanded Boggan to murder Richards, promising that, if he failed to kill him, he would do so himself; and the preparation which he was making to go to Cheraw strengthens the spuposition that such was the purport of the note which Boggan received from his father a few minutes before he committed the murder.

The Marshal died Friday morning, February 29th, after a week of intensest suffering.

Before the coroner's jury the surgeon who attended Richards testified as follows: "He was called Saturday, 23rd instant, at about 4:30 o'clock to see the deceased. Found him wounded in the left side with a pistol shot, between fourth and fifth ribs. Saw body of deceased at post mortem. Found, on opening the chest, large quantity of blood in cavity of lung. Left lung was wounded, and the ball then passed to the spinal column, which it shattered between fourth and fifth dorsal vertebrae."

William Henry Harrison Richards was a member of Company "G," Thirteenth Regiment Massachusetts Veteran Volunteers. He is said to have been a man well connected at home, and though, as stated in the early part of this sketch, much of his life in Cheraw was discreditable, yet, in his last hour of duty, he stood at his post and died as a man who has acted well his part.

Mr. Coward, the hapless young man who accidentally fell a victim to Boggan's reckless shooting, lingered for months on the verge of the grave, every part of his body below the wound being completely paralyzed. It was known from the ill-fated 23rd of February that he could not possibly survive, yet he kept cheerful to the end and bore his sufferings with sublime fortitude.

He was spared long enough to see his slayer called to an account for his misdeeds, and on Monday, the 2nd day of June, he quietly passed away, with a smile of recognition to his weeping friends, with the light of heaven in his eyes and a prayer of forgiveness upon his lips.

After the execution of his bloody work, Boggan Cash had had the brazen-faced audacity to give expression to the following sentiment, which is extracted from a letter addressed to a Cheraw gentleman, under date of February 27th: "I have no regret whatever for shooting Richards, and hope he may die."

It may be interesting to inquire into the causes which so far

JAMES COWARD,
Shot and killed by Boggan Cash, Feb. 23d, 1884.

debased a man, at one time considered most amiable by nature, until he could stealthily slip upon a foe from behind, slay him while making no effort to resist, and then declare, while his victim lay expiring, that he had no regret for what he had done.

To this end let us take up the life of Boggan Cash, and, tracing it with the hand of justice, let us divest our minds of all prejurice, and seek to discern the causes which produced deplorable results, and learn therefrom a beneficent lesson.

CHAPTER II.

Genealogy of the Cashes.

The paternal ancestor of the Cashes is unknown, and must be "guessed" at. About the time of the Revolutionary war, according to tradition, there came from the mountains of East Tennessee a person styling herself Mrs. Peggy Cash. She settled in Anson county, N. C., at or near the spot whereon the town of Wadesboro now stands. She had one son, of whom little is now known, save that he answered to the name of Ingoe Dozier Cash. He appears to have been a sort of lawyer, for, in a volume of the Supreme Court Reports from 1797 to 1806, printed in the year 1806, we find his name among other subscribing lawyers. Of his legal distinction, however, nothing is now known, and the opinion prevails among old citizens of Anson county who knew him, that, if he ever obtained license, he retired early from the practice of his profession.

From an old Family Bible now in my possession, printed during the last century, and which a connection (by marriage) of the Cash Family has loaned me, the following facts appear:

Ingoe Dozier Cash was born October 4th, 1767, and was married to Margaret Boggan, June 13, 1792.

Unto Ingoe Dozier Cash and his wife Margaret Cash (formerly Margaret Boggan) were born the following children:

Boggan Cash, born June 5, 1793.
Polly Cash, born January 9th, 1794.
James Dozier Cash, born October 27th, 1795.
Holden Wade Cash, born December 23, 1796.
Erwin Cash, born April 2nd, 1798.
William L. Thomas, (supposed natural son of Ingoe Dozier Cash by a strange woman) was born April 22, 1798.

MARRIAGES.—Boggan Cash, son of Ingoe Dozier Cash, was married to Elizabeth Ellerbe, Thursday, October 18, 1821.

Polly Cash was married to Thomas Ellerbe, Wednesday, November 8, 1809, in the 15th year of her age.

According to the Record there were no other marriages, but from the gentleman who loaned me the Family Bible above mentioned, I learn that James Dozier Cash, (second son of Ingoe Dozier Cash) was married to Miss Patsy May, of Chesterfield County, S. C.

DEATHS.—Ingoe Dozier Cash (the progenetor of the family,) died July 30, 1830, after a lingering illness, in the 64th year of his age.

Ervin Cash, son of Ingoe D. Cash, died in infancy, April 21st, 1798.

Holden Wade Cash, son of same, died October 21, 1821.

James Dozier Cash, son of same, died in 1865 or 1866, in about the seventieth year of his age.

William L. Thomas, who assumed the name of Thomas Cash, was killed in the neighborhood of Sneedsboro, near the South Carolina line, by Thomas Curtis, about the year 1835. He was acting as constable at the time, and attempted to arrest Curtis under a warrant which had expired, whereupon Curtis stabbed him to death with a knife. (Curtis was acquitted.)

Mrs. Polly Cash, (nee Polly Ellerbe) died July 31, 1824, in the 31st year of her age, leaving one son, Boggan Ellerbe, of whom mention will hereafter be made, and one daughter, Mary Ellerbe, who married Hunter Houze, of Franklin County, N. C., October 9th, 1829. After the death of her husband, Mrs. Houze taught school in Wadesboro, N. C., and from one of her pupils I learn that she went West with her children about the year 1844, after which all trace of her was lost.

Boggan Cash, the first son of Ingoe Dosier Cash, died Monday, the 14th of February, 1825, of typhus fever, in the 32nd year of his age. He left one son, Ellerbe Cash, who, after his father's death, added Boggan to his name.

This Ellerbe Cash is our present Col E. B. C. Cash, who, according to the Cash Family Record, is simply named Ellerbe Cash, and is in no sense entitled to the names "Boggan Crawford," both of which he assumed, the first many years ago and the latter one later in life.

The record ends here, but on excellent authority. I learned the facts set forth in the next chapter.

CHAPTER III.

Col. E. B. C. Cash.

E. B. C. Cash, or rightly, Ellerbe Cash, moved with his mother, Mrs. Elizabeth Cash, to Chesterfield county, S. C., the home of her girlhood, about the year 1837, where she owned considerable property inherited from her father.

Mrs. Cash was a very superior woman—a woman of intelligence and piety, but also of determination; and to the day of her death—which occurred since the late war—she swayed the scepter of authority over her too often erring son, Ellerbe. Ellerbe, however, be it said to his credit, was reverential to his mother and a most dutiful son.

When about twenty-four years of age he married Miss Alene E. Ellerbe, daughter of Dr. W. C. Ellerbe and Mrs. E. M. Ellerbe, of Kershaw county, S. C., in the month of November, 1848.

Unto Ellerbe Cash and his wife, Alene E. Cash, were born four children, viz., W. B. Cash, now deceased; Alene Cash, now Mrs. Watts, wife of Col. R. C. Watts, of Laurins, S. C.; Anna Cash, deceased; and Elizabeth Cash, the youngest, who is now in about her seventeenth year.

When a young man, Ellerbe Cash, or E. B. C. Cash, as we shall hereafter call him, that being the name which he assumed and by which he was known, studied law and obtained license to practice, but owing either to his inability to cope, in intellectual contests, with his brethren of the bar, or a distaste for the profession, he early abandoned it and devoted himself to mercantile and agricultural pursuits.

He was elected before the war to the Legislature, and represented Chesterfield county one term in that body. While there, he served his constituents with fidelity and to the best of his ability. He seems always to have had an inordinate desire for office, but the people of Chesterfield, for reasons satisfactory to themselves, saw fit to return him no more to the Legislature, and he was forced to seek solace in the Old Malitia, in which honorable organization he obtained a commission and won the title of " General !" which distinguished title he still bears with grace and dignity in his own county at least, if nowhere else.

Though possessed of magnificent estates, though hundreds of slaves responded to his every beck; though his home was the centre of hospitality and its doors open at all times to all comers, though the poor and the needy were never turned away empty; though he possessed abundant wealth which he expended with a lavish hand in the entertainment of his visitors;

though all who entered his home ever after praised his regal hospitality; though he had faithfully served his people in the councils of his adopted State; though he had acquired the distinguished cognomen of "General," still General Ellerbe Boggan Crawford Cash was never considered a South Carolina GENTLEMAN in the true acceptation of that term, and this fact has ever been to him his life's greatest bane. To him it was a source of mortification that he should not be considered one of the first gentlemen of his State. It was the skeleton at the feast, and tinctured with gall every cup of life's joy. He keenly felt a certain implied, if not expressed, sense of superiority on the part of the South Carolina gentry, and he was stung to the soul if there was ever an intimation of it, or the faintest semblance of superiority manifested toward him. Though he was far from being a man of fine sensibilities, yet he was sensitive in the extreme. He thought well of himself and wanted everybody else to do the same; but as he was lacking in those qualities which command respect and admiration, his impulse was to make up the deficiency by the exercise of brute force and to attain the same end by knocking down and dragging out every one who failed to recognize in him the typical Southern gentleman and the mirror of Southern chivalry.

When the talk of secession was first heard in the South, Gen. Cash was one of its pronounced and most vehement advocates. In all of South Carolina there was not a more unreasonable or a more blatant fire-eater—one who made louder boasts at home or who accomplished less in the line of duty when called to the front than did he. As a soldier he was noted for his cowardice, and as an officer he was distinguished for his tyranny. Indeed, so brutal was he, and such hatred did his acts inspire in the breasts of his subordinates, that he soon resigned his commission and left the army, to escape being shot by his own men. Before leaving the army, however, he procured a substitute in the person of John Gulledge, who was afterwards killed in Cash's place.

A gentleman of Chesterfield county—a dauntless wearer of the gray—who knows Col. Cash well, and who served under him, has furnished me with the following sketch:

"He was well known before the war as an extreme secessionist—a fire-eater, He was one of that class who promised to drink all the blood that would be spilled in the war. Certainly, then, he should have put his foot as far as any one to uphold the cause upon which the South staked everything. Did he do it? Let the facts answer:

"Early in 1861, the Eighth South Carolina Regiment was organized, and Gen. Cash was elected Colonel. The regiment saw its first service on the seaboard of our own State, and went early in the war to Virginia. Col. Cash was with his regiment at the first battle of Manassas on the 21st of July, 1861, and and at the battle of Williamsburg in 1862.

"At the organization early in 1862, he was not re-elected. He then came home and was never in any active service afterward, while those who served under him only grounded their arms when the Confederate flag went down.

"It is true that late in the war he was again elected Colonel of what was known as the "Reserves"—old men and boys—and for a few months did police duty on the coast.

"The only act by which Col. Cash gained any notoriety, so far as I know, occurred at the first battle of Manassas. Soon after pursuit commenced by our forces, we captured a gentleman in citizen's dress who proved to be Mr. —— Ely, a member of Congress from the State of New York. He was taken in charge by Captain John W. Harrington, of Company E. 8th South Carolina Regiment, and treated with every mark of courtesy due his rank and a prisoner of war. Captain Harrington introduced him to other officers, and no one treated him with any incivility untill he was introduced to Col. Cash. This gallant (?) Confederate officer immedtately drew his revolver and presented it at Mr. Ely, with a volly of oaths, declaring he intended to kill him. He chased Mr. Ely round and round Capt. Harrington, and afterwards round a tree, brandishing his pistol and abusing the unoffending gentleman, to the unbounded disgust and contempt of both the officers and men under his command."

ONE WHO SERVED UNDER HIM.

The above incident is characteristic of Col. Cash, and is sufficient to give every one a clear insight into the true nature of the man.

It would be unjust, however, to present this repulsive phase of Col. Cash's character, and not accredit him with whatever acts of generosity or humanity he is known to have performed.

Though his treatment to the men under him was in every sense reprehensible—brutal—still to the sick and wounded, and especially to the soldiers' needy families living in the vicinity of his home, he was gracious enough. Scarcely a train passed Cash's Depot that did not carry to the sick ones in the Charleston hospitals a profusion of stores—fresh meats, chickens, turkeys, butter, eggs, etc., and numberless delicacies well calculated to soothe and comfort the sufferers. When many heartless, mercenary men, who had shirked out of the army, were at home "speculating" in grain and provisions—often extortioning, oppressing—grinding to the earth the families of the men who were performing their duty at the front—often the widows and orphans of men who had fallen for their country—Col. Cash assumed a very different attitude, and whatever else may be said of him, in this particular, at least, he acted the part of a patriot and humanitarian. When some speculators were buying up—or seeking to buy up—all the grain in the country, that they might control the price of the same, Col. Cash at one time had in his granaries between 75,000 and 100,000 bushels of corn and wheat—held in reserve for the families of soldiers, and which he instructed his agents under no condition to dispose of to speculators. At that time corn and wheat sold for several dollars per bushel (Confederate money, of course,) but Col. Cash ordered that his grain should be disposed of only to poor families at not exceeding the nominal sum of 50 cents per bushel,—and when, as often happened, the needy ones had not the money wherewith to purchase, their wants were always supplied, and in not a single instance was a soldier's wife or child turned off without having their wants supplied.

Gladly would I dwell upon the man's good qualities, but as it is my purpose to deal only with the truth, I hasten on, and let the truth speak for itself.

After the war Col. Cash settled down on his plantation near Cash's Depot, and applied himself diligently to the repairing of whatever damages he may have sustained by the war. Foremost among the white men of his county was he in advocating the rule of South Carolina by white men, and not until long after the State government had passed from the hands of the negroes and the vandal legions who flocked to South Carolina during the days of reconstruction, did he act the traitor and give countenance to his former foes in their effort to again remand his State to Radical bondage and degradation.

It is possible that for the first few years after the war he did MORE for his people, in his zeal, than was incumbent upon a good citizen, and it is possible that the unbridled sway which he then allowed his patriotic impulses, may have played a considerable part in precipitating him into the lawless life which he has since led.

An idea may be formed of the tempest which raged in the man's breast by a few incidents which I have selected from a multitude that have been presented to my attention; although, in so doing, I do not mean to censure him too severely, for those were desperate days in South Carolina, and desperate measures may, in a degree, have been justifiable:

Soon after the Federal garrison was removed from Cheraw, two negroes, so the story runs, who had offended Col. Cash and sought the protection of the blue coats, were surreptitiously hanged on Col. Cash's premises. I do not vouch for the truth of this statement. It is told and believed in Chesterfield county, and it may or may not have been true, but if true it may have been excusable, for no one, save those who have lived through such a reign of anarchy as existed in some parts of the South, and particularly in South Carolina, when there were Federal bayonets present to encourage the negroes in lawlessness and to incite them to hostility to the whites, can appreciate what indignities many white men suffered at the hands of the misguided blacks.

On another occasion he is reported to have shot and killed his "head man"—his favorite servant—and if the circumstances, as reported to me, be correct, it was a most inexcusable crime. Col. Cash's horses were hid in the recesses of the Pee Dee swamps. The Yankees knew they were there but every search for them proved futile. Learning from some of the negroes less faithful than the old favorite, that he knew the whereabouts of the horses, they demanded of him that he lead them to the animals. The old darkey refused to comply, and only yielded when it became necessary to do so in order to save his life. For this, Col. Cash is said to have shot the faithful old darkey dead on sight.

Another negro, in his employ, displeased Col. Cash and was driven off the premises with the admonition to return no more under penalty of death. Some time afterwards he ventured to the "quarters" on a distant part of the Cash demesne. It so happened that Col. Cash rode by the quarters that day, and all of a sudden he came upon the intruder. The negro's knees knocked together, for the poor wretch thought his time had come. The Col. however, was not murderously inclined that day, so he merely spat in the darkey's face and forbid him to wipe it off, under threat of immediate death.

But Col. Cash did not always have things his own way. Sometimes the tables were turned upon him, as below: He had promised to kill an obsequious and very humble old darkey who had inadvertently offended him. Sambo avoided Col. Cash as he would the Arch Fiend himself, but one day when he was out squerril hunting, he chanced abruptly to meet Col. Cash in the swamps. The Colonel drew his pistol and smiled sardonically. Sambo trembled from head to foot, but a happy idea struck him and he darted into the bushes, fleeing for dear life. Col. Cash pursued. The negro, seeing that he was about to be overtaken, and feeling that he would be murdered, dodged behind a tree and leveled his musket at the Colonel, saying: "Stop dar, Mars Boggan an' doan' you come anudder step, or afor' God dis nigger will shoot you sartain to save hisself!"

It is useless to add that Col. Oash not only did heed the negro's admotion and stopped short off, but that he immediately remembered urgent business in another quarter and no further meddled with "the nigger behind the tree."

A short while after the occurrence of this incident, he tried, condemned, and sentenced five other negroes to be hanged at one time. He had these negroes swung up, and was in the act of letting the drop fall when Robert G. Ellerbe, his much-feared brother-in-law, for whom a messenger had been dispatched, rode up and put an end to the performance by threatening to hang Col. Cash himself if he did not desist.

On another occasion he hung two other seditious negroes, and below is given Col. Cash the benefit of his own explanation, and, if he speaks truthfully, every good citizen should commend the act. Says the Colonel:

"A detachment of Wheeler's cavalry were going through the country and playing off as Yankees. Two negroes went to them and told them that they proposed to burn out their owners and others, and other crimes they intended to commit. The cavalrymen at once notified the owners of the incendiary intention of the negroes, and it was determined by a large body of citizens to hang them and it was done. Who would have protested? For God's sake, I hope no man in South Carolina, no matter what else he condemns me for, would disapprove of my action in protecting our wives and children from the incendiary and the assassin."

There is, however, the blood of one more man on the hands of Col. Cash—the blood of a poor beggar, murdered upon his door-step—which is the least justifiable of any of his crimes.

However, let him have the benefit of his own testimony before giving the espression of the people of Chesterfield county, who tell a different tale. Says Col. Cash:

"The deceased was one of Henry Berry Lowery's gang of outlaws, and the killing of him was praised by everybody."

In this particular Col. Cash either wilfully or unconsciously makes a misstatement. When he shot the man he might have believed him to be one of the Swamp Angels, but such he could not have been, since the Lowery gang were all negroes and mongrels, while the party killed was a white man.

One of Col. Cash's friends has informed me that Col. Cash heard a noise at his front door, that he peeped through a window, and, when he saw the man, fired upon him without hailing him. The beggar fell with a groan an expired immediately. His name was never ascertained, there was nothing upon his person to tell who he was or whence he came, and no clue as to his identity has ever been obtained.

Had it not been for the evidence of a mulatto girl—Col. Cash's daughter, I am informed—who testified to an extraordinary tale before the Coroner's jury, Col. Cash would doubtless have suffered for his crime. At that time, as now, Col. Cash lived in dread of assassination. His life had been threatened by the Freemen brothers, a family of desperate men, between whom and himself there existed a deadly feud. (The last one of the Freemans, six or seven in all, are now serving out terms in the South Carolina penitentiary.) The threats which they were known to have made served Col. Cash admirably in escaping the penalty of his crime, and this, added to the testimony of the girl above mentioned, enabled him to escape without even so much as a hearing before the courts. The testimony before the Coroner's jury was about as follows:

"Col. Cash went to the door in response to a rapping. Just as he opened the door a pistol was fired in the yard a few steps distant. At the moment the pistol was fired, Col. Cash descried the man on his steps, and instantly fired upon him, supposing him to be one of the Freemans."

The evidence appearing positive that Col. Cash had acted in self defence, and had done nothing amiss, the grand jury failed to find a true bill against him and the matter was dropped.

Up to the year '76, nothing unusual seems to have transpired in the life of Col. Cash worthy of mention, but during that year, when the people of South Carolina determined to throw off the Radical yoke, he was one of the foremost men of the State in espousing the good work, and no one who saw him then could have believed it possible that in so short a period as six years would he be allied with that same party—strenuously endeavoring to reinstate that party in power.

It is impossible to conceive of his enthusiasm, or to form a just idea of his zeal, but I will cite an act or two of his during that year, and the reader may for himself judge of Col. Cash's devotion to the Democratic party—to the white man's party in South Carolina. In that year he surrendered his entire estate—some 7,000 or 8,000 acres—rent free to the freedmen, in consideration of their voting the Democratic ticket. In that year he gave thousands of dollars to advance the interests of the Democratic party, he chartered a train on the Cheraw & Darlington R. R. to carry Democratic voters to the various voting precincts along that road. All this the offering of one man—a man governed, one time at least, let us hope, by the purest and best motives.

It seems hard—it seems unjust—that a man who has done so much for his party should at any time be almost wholly deserted and denounced by his party; and if this be true in the case of Col. Cash, the cause of this revulsion must be sought in his own subsequent acts.

In this same eventful year Boggan Cash completed his studies and returned home to be his father's future companion and counselor. The lives of these two men so soon blend together that we must pause awhile here and consider the life of the younger Cash, before continuing that of the elder.

CHAPTER IV.

The Blood of Boggan Cash, as Transmitted from the Cashes and the Ellerbes.

> My ancient but ignoble blood,
> Has crept through scoundrels ever since the flood.
> —BURNS.

There is as much in the blood of men as there is in the blood of horses. When there is "bad blood" in a family it will crop out generation after generation; and when there is a vicious or criminal taint in the blood, the evil tendencies can rarely, and with greatest difficulty, be eliminated. When a man inherits evil propensities from his father, no one should be surprised if he develops evil traits of character; but when he inherits evil instincts from both sides of the ancestrial house, who can hope that he will not develop into a criminal?

In the case of Boggan Cash this was eminently true. There was bad blood in the man's veins—blood that had coursed through criminal veins for generations. The Cashes on the one side and the Ellerbes on the other, have been known throughout this region for more than a hundred years as vicious, desperate, criminal men.

In the year 1868 the Anson County Court-House was burned, and in the conflagration was destroyed every vestige of the criminal records of the county. But for this fact I might be able to make a terrible showing against the Cashes when they lived in this county. In the absence of undisputed testimony to bear me out in the assertion, I must omit the mention of many things which would speak against them.

However, in the old Cash family before mentioned, I find a document which helps to establish the fact that a long time ago the ancestor of the Cashes was acquainted with the county jail. The document in question reads:

James R. Black vs. Ingoe D. Cash,	Bill of Costs	-	-	$34.00
	JAILOR'S FEES PAID,	-	-	10.00
				$24.00

I must omit much of this nature which belongs to tradition, but will cite a few incidents in the lives of these men, of which I have been informed by old and trustworthy citizens of Anson county, now living, and which will suffice to show that they were by nature bad men:

When a young man Ingoe Dozier Cash lived with his mother at the "Buck Tavern," an old and dilapidated building still standing in Wadesboro, but unoccupied and forever deserted. On one occasion Ingoe went home intoxicated and raised a row with his mother. Now, Mrs. Cash was a large, sinewy, muscular woman, and—not afraid of any man. She caught Ingoe by the nape of his neck and the seat of his pantaloons and cast him headlong into the street from a second story porch. When Ingoe arose he shook his fist at the old lady and damned her well, after which he went back up town, swearing he was the "best man in Anson and could lick any man in Wadesboro."

Ingoe's son Boggan, the father of Col. Cash, was a "chip of the old block," but he has been dead now for nigh unto sixty years and most of his deeds are forgotten.

James Dozier Cash, however, another son, lived until about twenty years ago, and is still remembered by the people of Wadesboro. He was a notorious drinking man, a horse-racer, cock-fighter and a bruiser. In statue he was very low and chunky, with a head and neck like a Durham bull. He delighted in fighting and was never known to be whipped—except by his wife. It was his custom, whenever he got into a fight, to fall upon his back and fight from the bottom, and the man on top would invariably beg somebody to "please take him off Mr. Cash." His wife, however, was his boss, and often, when Dozier would go to the Buck Tavern, get drunk and remain out late, did Mrs. Cash hunt up the truant one and cowhide him home. Late in life he deserted his lawful spouse and took up with a negro woman, and from this unholy alliance originated the present Cash negroes of Wadesboro.

Col. E. B. C. Cash, when a young man, was also a bully and was ever seeking an opportunity for the display of his prowess. Soon after he removed to South Carolina, he heard of John Purvis, then living at or near Cheraw. Purvis was no bully, did not pride himself on his muscle, and was disposed at all times to avoid a difficulty. He was known, however, as a man of "grit," whom no one cared to "walk on." Of this enviable reputation, Ellerbe Boggan Crawford Cash determined to deprive him. He knew that he could lick Purvis because Purvis was a so much smaller man than himself. He sought an opportunity of putting his pet design into execution, and at last an opportunity offered. One day he found Purvis in a crowd and at once set to work to pick a row with him. Purvis being an easy, quiet, peaceable man, walked away. Soon Cash followed him up and renewed his persecutions. The Purvis' "dander" began to rise. He told Cash that he wanted no trouble with him, but that if nothing else would serve him, why, "Pitch in!" Cash pounced upon Purvis with a vengeance, but the latter "took care of himself," and, striking out like a battering ram, planted him a solid blow between the eyes and sent him winding like a spinning wheel some fifteen feet away. Thoroughly exasperated and foaming with rage, Cash picked himself up and again started for Purvis, who, again striking "straight out" from the shoulder, knocked Cash clear of the ground and sprawled him out at his full length. Cash was then satisfied, and from that time to the present he has never meddled with Johnny Purvis.

The Ellerbes, on the other hand, were even worse, if possible, than the Cashes, but a similar fate having befallen the criminal records of Chesterfield that befell the records of Anson, absolutely authentic information on many points that have come to my attention, is lacking, and I must therefore pass over much which could not fail to interest the general reader.

I have authentic information, however, for the following brief summary of their violent deeds:

Thomas Ellerbe, brother of Dr. Ellerbe, who was Boggan Cash's great uncle, quarreled with a Lincoln county (N. C.) wagoner, near Cheraw, and in the quarrel struck him over the head with a plank. The wagoner was killed, and Thomas Ellerbe fled to Florida to escape the penalty of his crime. In Florida he quarreled with one of his own sons, whom he murdered, and again did he flee the country to escape the consequences. He next went to Raleigh, N. C., where he was recognized, apprehended, carried back to South Carolina and tried for his life, fifteen years after the commission of his first crime. He was sentenced to the penitentiary for three years, and after serving out his term, came to North Carolina and settled near Rocky River Springs, in what was then Montgomery (now Stanly) county, where he married a second time.

A son of this Thomas Ellerbe, Boggan Ellerbe by name, was a terror throughout this region, although I fail to learn of any murder that he ever committed. In those peaceful days, when men lived in amity, Boggan Ellerbe traveled with two pistols and a Bowie knife buckled around him, and "slept upon his arms" at all times. On one occasion he came to Wadesboro especially to kill his uncle Dozier Cash, whom he had loaned $20, and which Dozier was tardy in repaying. Cash kept a bar-room. Ellerbe, mounted on his horse, charged into the bar-room with both pistols drawn, "threatening vengeance on the head of Dozier," who leaped through a window to save his life. A gentleman now living in Wadesboro, and from whom I learned the particulars of this performance, prevented Ellerbe from murdering his uncle by assuming the debt himself and at once paying the $20.

Mrs. Mary Houze, before mentioned, was the sister of this Boggan Ellerbe.

Dr. W. C. Ellerbe, Boggan Cash's grandfather, was also a violent man, but he assumed to be something of a refined rough. He preferred to have his colored coachman do his fighting for him. Once he quarreled with May Buchanan, of Anson county, and then caused his man to horse-whip Buchanan until his coat was cut to shreds and his back lacerated till the blood streamed from it. Dr. Ellerbe and Col. Cash stood by and witnessed the whipping. The servile Buchanan accepted $500 for injuries sustained and the matter was dropped as far as he was concerned, but the negro was afterwards caught in North Carolina and adequately punished at the whipping post for the part he had taken in the chastisement of Buchanan.

Napoleon Ellerbe, a son of Dr. Ellerbe, also a notorious rough and rowdy, left home when quite a young man and has not been heard from in almost a quarter of a century. True to his name and his instincts he may long ere this have "died in his boots."

Zach Ellerbe, a cousin of Dr. Ellerbe, quarreled with his son Calhoun, rushed upon him with a knife and stabbed him to death. He afterwards shot and killed a little negro boy, for which he was sent to the penitentiary.

There is much more charged to the account of the Ellerbes which I must pass over, but this record of their crimes should be sufficient to establish the fact that they were monstrous people, and it cannot be wondered at that from a union of two such families as the Cashes and the Ellerbes a race of desperate criminals should spring.

Having thus shown the natural pre-disposition to crime which was planted in Boggan Cash when he became a "living being," let us trace his life through boyhood up to manhood, and discern, if we may, if he be not more entitled to commiseration than to censure. Let us place the blame where it belongs, and drop a tear of pity upon the sod which covers this "grey-eyed man of destiny."

CHAPTER V.

William Boggan Cash.

W. B. Cash was born in Chesterfield county, S. C., November 9th, 1855, and was therefore in the 29th year of his age when he died.

His troubles appear to have commenced almost with his birth, or very soon thereafter. When he was about one year old, his father was so cruel to his mother that the unhappy lady was forced to leave her home and seek the protection of her brothers, Robert G. and Napoleon Ellerbe, who lived with their mother, Mrs. E. M. Ellerbe, in Kershaw county, S. C.

Mrs. Cash was an invalid, suffering with a spinal affection, and had to be conveyed to her mother's home on a mattress. When she reached her mother's, the mattress was rudely deposited on the floor, and Col. Cash, who had accompanied her, demanded, in a savage voice, to know when he should come for her. Conscious of her security, she replied, "Never! I am at home once more and here I intend to remain—never again shall I be your slave."

Cash was enraged, but he dreaded the wrath of his wife's brothers too much to evince his displeasure and at once left the premises, with instructions no more to show his face in that quarter, which instructions he obeyed for a year or two, fearing to encounter Mrs. Cash's brothers, who had sworn vengeance upon him, did he again dare to wrong their sister.

At last, however, he determined to have Mrs. Cash return to his home, and he decided upon the following ignominious device for causing her to do so:

He ventured to within a few hundred yards of the Ellerbe mansion and secreted himself in the woods. Then, raising his glasses, he surveyed the premises from his ambush until he saw the Ellerbes leave. Stealthily he advanced upon the house and entered it—entered the house he dared not approach until it was left in the possession of defenceless women, one of them his invalid wife!

Little Boggan was sporting on the floor near his mother. Taking the little one in his arms, he abruptly informed Mrs. Cash that she could follow him or let it alone, just as she liked, but that he intended to have the child; whereupon he walked off, carrying the baby with him.

Of course the poor woman could do nothing but follow her tyrant lord, just as any other mother would have done under similar circumstances. It is possible that Col. Cash, after, by

W. B. CASH.

As he appeared at the Va. Mil. Institute in 1873.

most ignoble strategy, causing Mrs. Cash to return to his home, was less cruel to her, for a time, than he had been formerly. At any rate they lived together for a number of years, but at last Mrs. Cash was again forced to seek refuge in the home of her mother. The second separation continued for several years, and no doubt would have lasted for all time, had not Col. Cash again employed most dastardly means of forcing her to return. He went to Camden where one of his little girls was attending school. Watching his chances he caught her when no one was nigh to answer her cries or to rescue her from the man at whose hands her poor mother had suffered so much. She was taken home with her father without being allowed to see her mother. Of course Mrs. Cash could do nothing but again return to her husband, or suffer the child to grow up under the ungodly influence of her father.

I regret to thus invade the privacy of a man's home and drag the family skeleton forth to the light of day, I would not do so, did I not have an object in view which will hereafter be indicated.

Let us now return to the boy Boggan. His early years passed away, of course, with the occurrence of little, if anything, worth recording here; although, at that tender period, the character of the future man was being formed. Two adverse influences were then being brought to bear upon that character: The evil influence of an evil father and the salutary influence of a Christian mother. Whatever there was in the character of Boggan Cash admirable or lovable, was due to her care. It has been shown how he inherited a depraved and loathsome nature from his ancestors, and as it must be admitted, even by his enemies, later in life, that there was something positively lovable about the man, that lovable feature can be attributed only to education and not to inheritance.

The question may be asked here: "If the Ellerbes were all such evil people, how could Boggan Cash's mother have been a good woman?"

In answer, I can only say, "I know not, I cannot understand; but I know such to be a fact, and that I have observed many other similar instances—instances where the male members of a family have been vicious and worthless, but where the female members have been pure and good. It seems that the Almighty, to prevent man from sinking to total depravity, has created the female part of the world infinitely better than the male, and I have long marked the contrast which exists in this particular, between the sexes. All, or nearly all, the honesty, the virtue, the goodness, which there is in this world, is representented by the women. I do not know that any one, especially in the chivalric South, will dispute this, but it may be done, and I may be pointed to the outcast women of the world; I may have my attention called to the depths of ignominy to which women sometimes sink—to the revolting crimes which have been committed by women. Let it be so. I still contend that all, or nearly all, the good which there is in this world is represented by the women, and without pausing to argue how the vicious and the criminal part of womankind may have become so through man's instrumentality, I cite the cavaler's attention to one extraordinary fact, viz: According to the police reports of our great cities, only one per cent. of all the crimes committed are committed by the women, while the other 99 per cent. are committed by men. These figures speak a tale for the women which no sort of reasoning can refute. I have shown how the Cashes and the Ellerbes were bad men, but I have yet to hear of the first female member of either family who was not a pure, virtuous, good woman; and this may answer the seeming enigma, "How Boggan Cash could inherit bad blood from both ancestors and still have a pure, holy Christian mother."

Early in life he was started to school to Miss Mary Hawes, a maiden lady who still lives within about two miles of Cash's Depot. After leaving Miss Hawes' he went to school in Sumter and in Charleston. He entered Bingham School in August, '71, and there remained till June, '72. A letter from Major Bingham, addressed to myself, contains a pleasant and complimentary allusion to him. True, as I learn from Major Bingham's letter, "he was not especially studious, but he was quiet and orderly, and was a favorite with teachers and pupils. He showed nothing of the characteristics which have developed since and which are a surprise to all who knew him."

The press of the country has been most unjust to Boggan Cash. It has censured him in many instances without knowing whereof it has spoken, and has made charges against him which have contained no element of truth. A paper now before me states, and the statement continues to go the rounds of the press: "Nature formed him for a desperado. When a boy he was cruel and treacherous, and with each year he became more hardened and vicious, and shortly after he left the University of Virginia he killed a man in a street fight."

This is false in nearly every particular. Boggan Cash never attended the University of Virginia and he never killed a man in a street fight. If, "each succeeding year he became more hardened and vicious," it was not until after he became a man, more than 21 years of age.

There is some truth in the statement that "Nature formed formed him for a desperado," but it was the force of circumstances that developed him into such a character after he became a man.

That he was "cruel and treacherous when a boy," is most unjust—most false.

He was as kind and tender of heart as any boy could be, and was gentle almost to effeminacy. Several of my friends were with Boggan at Bingham's, and they are unanimous in this statement. One of my most intimate friends roomed with Boggan, and he cannot find terms sufficiently warm to praise his goodness of heart, his amiability, his generosity, and his devotion to his friends.

In the light of subsequent events, it is bad enough to speak the truth of Boggan Cash, without charging him with cruelty and treachery when a boy—the two meanest instincts that ever existed in the breast of a man or woman.

After leaving Bingham's in June '72, he entered the Virginia Military Institute in the fall following, where he remained four years, graduating July 1876, with the highest military honors—that of Captain.

I met Boggan Cash in the month of January, 1877, and never before nor since have I met a more prepossessing or a more magnetic person, nor one, perhaps, whom I shall remember longer—whom I shall remember with emotions so strangely blended with pleasure, with regret, with indignation, with disdain.

But let a further review of the man's life be continued in another chapter.

CHAPTER VI.

Boggan Cash Returns to his Home after the Completion of his College Days.

When Boggan Cash returned to his home after the completion of his studies in the year 1876—that year so memorable in the annals of South Carolina—he gave promise of a successful life, a life fraught with joy to himself and full of usefulness to others.

In person, he was exceedingly handsome. His manners were polished and courtly. His sensibilities were apparently as fine and delicate as a woman's. His mind was active, if not strong and vigorous. And to all these endowments and acquirements was added a thorough education, gained in the best schools of the county. The homes of the best families in that region were open to him, and in them he was a frequent, welcome visitor. He was esteemed by the men for his seeming sterling qualities, and admired by the ladies for his handsome person, his smooth tongue, his soft words of flattery—and, perhaps, for his wealth.

At all events he was "courted and caressed," and was universally regarded as a "coming man."

In less than eight years from that season of promise we see Boggan Cash an outlaw—a fugitive from justice—a crimson-handed murderer—a despised assassin, shrinking from public sight, and hidihg in the swamps to avoid arrest for his crimes and to escape the gallows. We see him at last hunted down by the officers of the law—surrounded by an armed body of men—fleeing and fighting with desperate valor as he flees. We see him a bloody corpse—shot to death by the officers of the law—pierced by a score or more of leaden balls—pierced through the brain and through the heart—shot from behind and before—riddled. We see the pampered child of fortune and of wasted opportunities stretched upon the ground lifeless and gory—left for hours unattended—his contorted limbs and pallid features blistering beneath the Southern sun. We see ants and spiders crawling over the lifeless body of the slain murderer, while myriad flies swarm around his corse—with no loving hand to care for the mortal remains of that once loving and lovable, but hapless, erring child of destiny!

Was there ever before anything just like it? I think not. If it be asked, "How could a man, whose prospects were so promising as were Boggan Cash's in 1876, come to such an end in 1884, I answer that he was lacking in the essential, the fundamental qualities of manhood—that the qualities which the world saw were only acquired—artificial—and not real; that by instinct he was a bad man, but that early and judicious training, on the part of his mother, had for a time deflected his natural bent; that when manhood was attained and he felt no longer the necessity of obeying the councils of his mother, who had so long guided the footsteps of his boyhood, he naturally "fell into line" with his father, whose precepts and whose example so well accorded with his own inclinations.

In the year 1876 we see Boggan Cash freed from the thraldom of the school room. We see him his own man, returned to the home of his boyhood. We see him nestling once more in the embrace of father, mother and sisters. We see him happy, or apparently so, at least.

Draw near, reader, and let us ascertain, in the next chapter, if Boggan Cash were really happy—if happiness were possible in the home which recognized in Col. Cash its lord and sovereign.

CHAPTER VII.

Boggan Cash at Home.

Shortly after his return from the Virginia Military Institute, Boggan Cash, in the home of his innocent childhood, became an actor in a most disgusting domestic drama, although the part he played was commendable enough.

When he returned home he found his father living with a negro mistress, and, if I am correctly informed, under the same roof which sheltered his long-suffering mother.

Whether this state of affairs were new to him I know not. I incline to the belief, however, from information which has come to me, that it was no new thing, but that Col. Cash, as he grew older, becoming more and more depraved, became more public and unblushing in his abominations. I incline to the belief, also that Boggan, until he became a man, had not the temerity to reproach his father or condemn the old man's iniquity. At any rate, as I am informed upon what I deem trustworthy authority, Boggan Cash saw his mother day after day insulted, humiliated, and subjected to the most revolting indignities at the hands of his father's concubine. At last, thoroughly exasperated, his blood boiling with indignation, Boggan, in his father's presence, said to Mrs. Cash: "Mother, this is no place for you. Come with me and I will take you away from these disgusting scenes."

Mrs. Cash, finding a champion in her boy, readily assented, and mother and son were in the act of departing when Col. Cash's ever-ready pistol was drawn upon Boggan and the drama came near ending in a tragedy.

Col. Cash gives as an excuse that he was afraid Boggan, in his rage, would shoot him, and hence he "got the drop" upon him. Let Col. Cash have the benefit of this excuse. I cannot see that it justifies the act.

Boggan, instead of carrying his project into execution, as he should have done, agreed upon a compromise with his father, and it was decided that he and his mother should remain.

After this, Col. Cash, a very magnetic man, soon acquired an absolute ascendency over Boggan, which it appears he had lost, in a measure, while the latter was at school, and soon Boggan's individuality was lost in him.

Col. Cash's control was absolute and his will sovereign law. We never again hear of Boggan expressing an opinion of his own or contesting a single point with his father. It was his part to obey, without questioning why.

Side by side and hand in hand, we ever after see them—the father sinning and the son conniving—the son sinning and the father nodding assent. Soon we see the former amiable man indulging in the most frightful excesses, as if the pent-up energy of a life-time would exhaust itself in an hour.

It would be tedious and disgusting to trace his life through its winding mazes at that time, as we find Boggan Cash descending the steps of vice and crime. A few instances must suffice.

In the year 1878 he fought a duel with Miller Williams, of Camden, S. C.

The causes of this duel were as farcical as the duel itself, and too obnoxious too mention here. Williams and Cash met, just over the line in North Carolina, about a dozen miles from Wadesboro. The duel(?) was the veriest child's play. Blank cartrides were used and of course nobody was hurt.

Mr. John Cantey, of Camden, was Williams second. He seems to have been so thoroughly disgusted with the affair that he was unspairing in his ridicule of it.

Boggan, feeling that his honor (?) was damaged, and that nothing would repair the injury save another farce, challenged Mr. Cantey, who, like an idiot, accepted the challenge and a second meeting was agreed upon, which came off at DuBoise's Bridge, Darlington county, S. C., (near the famous Cash-Shannon duel ground) in the spring of 1879. Blank cartridges were again used and again nobody was hurt.

Some morbid sentimentalists have sought to create a sympathy for Boggan Cash by endeavoring to make it appear that his downfall was attributable to an unfortunate affair ot the heart; that, like Jean Lafeitte, who, in the early part of the present century, being "crossed in love," left his South Carolina home to become the most noted pirate of the Gulf, Boggan Cash, for a similar cause, became a desperado because his affections, bestowed upon a certain lady, were not requited.

With such stuff, I have but little patience, and vile as Boggan Cash proved himself to be, I am at least glad to say for him that he was not such a consummate simpleton as some of his friends would make him appear in the eyes of all sensible men and women.

His affections were not unrequited. He loved, or thought he loved, a very amiable and accomplished lady, whose name I withhold, for the reason that, to mention it in connection with Boggan Cash, could not fail to pain and humiliate her.

It is needless to go into the details of this unfortunate affair (unfortunate for the lady, I mean.) I will only state that she loved Boggan Cash a thousand times more than he deserved, but that the ladys father, feeling himself in dutybound to guard the peace of his child, interposed and pre-

vailed upon her to postpone the marriage till after his death.
The prudent old man made no mistake. He felt assured, judging by the speed with which Boggan Cash was stepping downward, that if the marriage were postponed for a season it would never be solemnized—that Boggan Cash would change his mind or that his daughter would see the folly of uniting her destiny with his.

Ordinarily, my observation teaches me, young people should be allowed to settle their matrimonial affairs without the intervention of others. My observation teaches me also that the "making of matches" by parents and others is almost invariably followed by unhappy consequences; but my observation teaches me, also, that in the majority of cases, when a parent opposes the marriage of a child to a questionable character, through solicitude for that child's happiness, and not from a sordid motive, the parent is generally right. Indeed, nine-nine times out of a hundred the parent IS right, and the child will do well to act in obedience to the parent's counsel.

Never was this more faithfully illustrated than in the case of Boggan Cash and his affianced, and the example I commend to all wayward young people whose impetuosity urges them to ignore paternal prayers and entreaties.

The father of the young lady knew that his child could never be happy with Boggan Cash, and prevailed upon her, as above stated, to postpone the marriage until after his death. She acquiesced, not without a struggle, truly, but she acquiesced, nevertheless.

Note the sequel. The father lived only about a year or two thereafter, when his daughter was free to do as she liked. Though she still loved Boggan Cash, yet let us believe her discretion would forever have prevented her from marrying him, had Boggan renewed his suit; which, however, he failed to do.

Col. Cash, it seems, actuated by a spirit of retaliation, had either weaned Boggan away from his love, or so inflamed his mind with resentment against the hapless girl's father, that, after the father's death, he made no overtures for a reconciliation during the two years which intervened between the death of his once-betrothed's father and his own death.

Boggan Cash figured in one or two other affairs of the heart —or of passion—but the particulars are too ridiculous to enlist the reader's attention, and I shall therefore pass them by without notice.

At the time these events were transpiring, Boggan Cash was retrograding in morals and in the esteem of his friends and acquaintances about as fast, it would appear, as it is possible for a young man to retrograde, but he did not reach the steepest declivity along the line of his descent, until sometime later, as we shall presently see.

All long, Col. Cash was his companion, his friend, his counselor—his evil genius—in whom, as has been stated, Boggan seems to have lost his own identity. Never was his father known to rebuke him for a single excess, and never was he known to pause for a moment in his insane course and counsel his son to a life of virtue and of purity.

On they plunged, father and son, into the depths of the most appalling sins, until we find both guilty of the infernal crime of incest (with their mulatto daughter and sister) and uniting all of their hellish energies in goading to desperaton an unoffending gentleman that an excuse might be offered for murdering him— that they might murder him to gratify a malign spirit—all under the pretext of vindicating wounded honor.

Allusion is here made, as the people of Chesterfield understand and dare not deny, to the mulatto woman, Juliana, who is Col. Cash's daughter, and of whom mention will again be made, and to the Cash-Shannon trouble, and that Col. Cash and his son may no longer find a single honest sympathizer, I will hereafter tell as much of their connection with Juliana as a sense of decency will warrant, and will now tell the exact truth— so little understood—of the DuBois Bridge tragedy. I have labored long and patiently in gathering all obtainable data, and have honestly striven to present the facts in a manner that every one can understend, which are faithfully, fearlessless set forth in the next chapter.

CHAPTER VIII.

The Cash-Shannon Duel.

Much has been written on the subject of the Cash-Shannon duel, but the exact facts are little understood. All of the newspaper reports which have come under my eyes, though in many instances full and comprehensive, have yet left me in doubt on one important point. Col. Cash, a few years ago, published a pamphlet—his own version—but that did not clear up the mystery. The excuse of Col. Cash, for seeking a hostile meeting with the unfortunate Shannon, was that Shannon had charged his wife with fraud. Let that item be remembered.

After a careful, patient, thorough investigation of the subject—determined to sift matters to the bottom—I have arrived at the conclusion that there was a fraud, or "family arrangement," as it was designated, and I so assert it in the beginning, but repudiate the idea, at the same time, that poor Mrs. Cash was responsible for it.

Had W. L. DePass, who first made the charge, possessed sufficient manhood to express his convictions and to stand up to them, the noble but hapless Shannon might to-day be living.

But I anticipate my narrative. The main facts which I shall set forth have been so often recounted that many who will read this pamphlet are already familiar with them, and I must therefore crave their indulgence while I seek to array the same facts before them again, but in a different shape, I trust, from that in which they have hitherto been presented, believing, as I do, that all will join with me in saying that the charges of DePass, which ended in the death of Shannon, were true, and only needed to be fearlessly pressed in oder to have their truth established in opinion of every fair-minded person :

About the year 1874, Robert G. Ellerbe, a notorious rough and bully of Kershaw county, S. C., assaulted one Conrad M. Weinges, an old and respected citizen of said county. Weinges sustained serious bodily injuries at the hands of Ellerbe.

On the 9th of December, 1878, Weinges commenced an an action for damages against said Ellerbe in the Court of Common Pleas for the county of Kershaw. Anticipating that damages might be recovered, and to escape paying the same, Ellerbe, on the 27th of January following, (1879) confessed judgment to his sister, Mrs. Alene E. Cash, in the sum $15.000.

The case, Weinges vs. Ellerbe, was tried at the September term of the Court of Common Pleas, in the year 1879, and recovered $2,000 damages, together with costs and disbursements of said plaintiff, sixty-three dollars and five cents (in all $2,063.05), and the Sheriff of said county in October 1879, was directed to levy upon and sell the real and personal property of said Robert G. Ellerbe, and out of same satisfy said judgment.

That Robert G. Ellerbe was really indebted to Mrs. Cash I believe is possible, but that the judgment was confessed to her to escape paying the damages afterwards recovered by Weinges I believe is equally true, as I will presently show, and that it would never have been confessed, except in anticipation that Weinges would recover damages, I believe is also true, as I will endeavor further to show.

I now ask the reader to keep in view the foregoing facts while considering the following statement made by Col. Cash under oath, showing or pretending to show, how Robert G. Ellerbe came to be indebted to Mrs. Cash in the sum of $15,000. The reader can then judge whether or not it were a just debt:

Col. Cash states that at the time of his marriage, in 1848, "Mrs. Cash was entitled to an undivided interest in the lands of her father's estate as her share therein, as well as a number of slaves. That Mrs. Cash got the slaves in possession soon after their marriage, but that the lands of the estate and the crop of the year 1848, was left there. That the heirs of Dr. W. C. Ellerbe (Mrs. Cash's father), were his widow, Mrs. E. M. Ellerbe, Mrs. Alene E. Cash, W. C. S. Ellerbe and Napoleon Ellerbe. That W. C. S. Ellerbe married the same year and left the homestead; and that Napoleon Ellerbe has not been heard from in twenty years. That when Mrs. Cash was married in 1848, Robert G. Ellerbe was a young man about eighteen or nineteen years old, and remained on the place until the present time (1880) using the stock (except the horses and mules, which had been divided off) and the agricultural implements, and has continued to do so from that day to the present time, never paying his sister, Mrs. Cash, during the whole period of thirty-one years, more than five hundred dollars on account thereof. * . That he had used and appropriated the whole profit to himself. That the entire plantation consisted of about thirteen hundred acres, more or less, all of which was arable, except about one hundred acres in woodland; and that Robert G. Ellerbe worked on said land a considerable number of slaves up to 1865, and had most of the plantation in cultivation the entire time. That Robert G. Ellerbe held the lands, stock, and all other property of their mother, Mrs. E. M. Ellerbe, in his possession during the entire period, and used and enjoyed the proceeds and profits arising therefrom without ever paying anything for it. - - That the confession of said judgment was given to secure what Robert G. Ellerbe owed his sister, Mrs. Cash, and his mother, on account of rents, arising from the use of their respective interests in these lands. - - In January, 1879, Robert G. Ellerbe visited his mother and his sister, Mrs. Cash—his mother then being living with Mrs. Cash in Chesterfield county—and while there the witness insisted on Robert G. Ellerbe making some arrangement to secure the said indebtedness which existed from him to his mother and sister. ☞ Robert G. Ellerbe reluctantly consented to it, because, as he said, he did not believe Weinges would press his suit to judgment. Witness believed that Weinges would press the suit, because he knew of such a case in Chesterfield. - - - Witness being well acquainted with the property, and the uses to which Robert G. Ellerbe had applied it, he and Ellerbe made a calculation of what his indebtedness to his mother and sister would be, and we soon found that it ran up to over twenty thousand dollars. That Ellerbe and witness thought it useless to expect so much to be paid out of the property of Ellerbe, and we agreed to fix the sum at fifteen thousand dollars. . . The statement and confession of judgment was the result. - - Witness had no personal claim of Mrs. Cash, but as she was his wife, he deemed it his duty to act for her in the matter, and she approved it. - - The reason why witness had never before looked after the interests of his wife in the estate of her father, was because he had a delicacy in mentioning the subject to R. G. Ellerbe: because that his wife had never needed it, she had plenty without and thought it safe. The reason why a confession of judgment was taken instead of a mortgage, was because Gen. Prince advised it."

I desire now to establish two points: 1st, that this was a "family arrangement, entered into between Robert G. Ellerbe and E. B. C. Cash to defeat the recovery of damages by Weinges," and 2nd, that unhappy Mrs. Cash was not responsible for it, and that her husband acted without her solicitation.

To establish the first point, I call to my aid Col. Cash himself, who above states, "That Robert G. Ellerbe reluctantly conseted to it—the confession of judgment—because, as he said, he did not believe Weinges would press the suit to judgment, but that he (Col. Cash) believed that Weinges would press the suit, because he knew of such a case in Chesterfield."

Could anything be more evident than that Robert G. Ellerbe confessed judgment to his sister, not to secure her in his reputed indebtedness, but to escape the payment of the judgment which Col. Cash felt assured Weinges would recover against said Ellerbe. Is not Col. Cash's statement a confession as plain as plain can be?

To establish the second point, I also call Col. Cash to witness, wherein he states above, that he "Had no personal interest in the claim of Mrs. Cash against Robert G. Ellerbe, and did not consult with Mrs. Cash."

Is it not plain that Col. Cash and Robert G. Ellerbe alone were responsible for the transaction, and that Mrs. Cash had no part in it? Is not Col. Cash's own statement an unmistakable confession?

As a further evidence I cite the testimony of Jack Saunders, under oath, who states that after the Weinges verdict, he met Robert G. Ellerbe, and that Ellerbe said to witness, "Jack, shall we fight or make friends? Said he was willing to pay Weinges something, but not the amount recovered. That Weinges' suing him had forced him to PAY DEBTS HE NEVER WOULD HAVE HAD TO PAY, AND NEVER INTENDED TO PAY."

I have before me Robert G. Ellerbe's own statement, under oath, but deem it unnecessary to present it here, as it is only a corroboration, in every particular, of Col. Cash's statement, given above, and would only occupy space without adding additional weight to the evidence, which is conclusive enough that the reputed confession of judgment was "a family arrangement," entered into by the parties above named and for the purposes above indicated.

Having satisfactorily established the two points, viz: That Robert G. Ellerbe and E. B. C. Cash entered into an arrangement for the purpore of defeating the recovery of damages by Weinges, and that Mrs. Cash was innocent of any part it, let us now proceed to a further consideration of the matter in hand, and next establish the fact that Col. Cash was inexcusable in seeking a meeting with Shannon—that he was influenced by a spirit of inexcusable malice—that he desired to murder one or both of the attorneys who unearthed his knavery, not to redress the wrongs which he alleges Mrs. Cash had suffered at their hands, but to sate a hellish spirit of revenge that was excited in his breast when he found himself checkmated in his villainy.

The reader will bear in mind now that there were two judgments against the property of Robert G. Ellerbe, the one obtained in the court of Common Pleas for Kershaw county, by Conrad M. Weinges, at the September term 1879, and the other, a confession of judgment, made by said Robert G. Ellerbe to his sister, Mrs. Alené E. Cash, on the fourteenth of February, 1870, to defeat the recovery of damages by said Weinges, which, Col. Cash believed would be recovered by Weinges, whenever the case should come up for trial.

The Court in which the case of Weinges vs. Ellerbe was to be tried convened on the ―― day of September, 1879. Col. Cash, knowing that Weinges would recover damages, and that his only security lay in expediting matters, on the 11 day of September, 1879 (after Weinges had recovered damages for $2,000,) ordered the Sheriff of Kershaw county to levy upon and sell the property of Robert G. Ellerbe, to satisfy the judgment which the said Robert G. Ellerbe had confessed to his sister, Mrs. Alene E. Cash.

On the same day that the order was given to the Sheriff of Kershaw county to levy upon and sell the property of Robert G. Ellerbe, to satisfy the judgment which said Ellerbe had confessed to his sister, Col. Cash was notified that the judgment held by Mrs. Cash would be contested by Col. William M. Shannon and W. L. DePass, attorneys representing Weinges, who held a junior judgment.

The property was duly advertised to be sold on the 2nd day of November, 1879. On that same day Col. Cash went to Camden to attend the sale, and the Sheriff informed him that the sale would be held at 12 M.

At the hour appointed for the sale the Sheriff waited upon Col. Cash and informed him that the sale would not take place, as he had just been served with an injunction forbidding the sale, "and with a summons and complaint against himself, Mrs. Cash and others."

In his pamplet Col. Cash says:

"I asked him (the Sheriff) for the use of his copy, and took it to the law office of Messrs. Leitner & Dunlap, and gave it to Major Leitner to read. ‑ ‑ From the reading I was satisfied a charge of fraud was intended, and I took a copy of the most offensive charge, which was a marginal note on the last page (no other part at that time struck me so forcibly at that time as the marginal note.)"

The marginal note in question, of which so much has been said, and which was Col. Cash's sole excuse for seeking a meeting with either of the attorneys representing Weinges, was as follows:

"That further the plaintiff alleges that the pretended confession of judgment has been made by said defendant, Robert G. Ellerbe, to his own sister, who is said Alene E. Cash, and thus, by a family arrangement, the said defendant intends to defeat the recovery of the plaintiff."

This was all, positively all, the excuse which Col. Cash could hatch up for seeking a meeting with either Col. Shannon or Captain DePass, as will subsequently be shown; and it will be shown, furthermore, that Col. Shannon was in no sense responsible for said charge.

The reader is requested to remember Col. Cash's statement, before given, and, remembering it, to reflect how like the truth sounds the marginal note which gave Col. Cash such deadly offence.

Conscious of his guilt, and furious that any one should have the termerity to make such a charge, Col. Cash sought no explanation, but a few days thereafter sent two challenges, one to Col. Shannon and one to Captain DePass. These challenges were entrusted to Boggan Cash, who was instructed to deliver them to certain parties in Columbia, who, in turn, were to deliver them to Messrs. Shannon and DePass, who, it was surmised, would both be in said city attending the State Fair, at the time Boggan was expected to arrive there. Failing to meet with Messrs. Shannon and DePass in Columbia, the challenges were to be delivered to them in Camden. It chanced that neither Col. Shannon nor Captain DePass were in Columbia, and hence the challenges could not be delivered immediately.

Boggan then conferred with Gen. Johnson Hagood—a man after Col. Cash's own heart—who took the challenges and submitted them to the gentlemen who were to deliver them to Messrs. Shannon and DePass. Each of these gentlemen, together with Gen. Hagood, wrote out his opinion disapproving of any action on the part of Col. Cash, so long as there was any issue at law, lest his motives might be misconstructsd.

I quote the above statement from Col. Cash's pamphlet, as I do the following: When the statements of Gen. Hagood and the gentleman above mentioned were received by Col. Cash, he was in Kershaw county, the home of Col. Shannon and Captain DePass. The day after the statements were received, mutual friends assured Col. Cash of Col. Shannon's kindly feeling toward himself, and a few days afterward Col. Cash addressed the following letter to Col. Shannon:

CASH' DEPOT, November 24th, 1879,

Colonel Wm. M. Shannon:

Colonel—I have seen the original summons and complaint of a case entitled Conrad M. Weinges sv. Allen E. Cash and others, in which your name appears as one of the attorneys for the plaintiff In the latter part of the instrument are the following words: "That further, the plaintiff alleges that the pretended confession of judgment has been made by said defendant, Robert G. Ellerbe, to his own sister, who is the said Allen E. Cash, and thus, by a family arrangement, the said defendant intends to defeat the recovery of plaintiff." These words are not in the body of the instrument, but are written on the margin of the summons, and may have been placed there after your signature had been affixed. These words have been erased on the copy served on Mrs. Cash's attorney. When I consider to kindly relations which have existed between us for more than twenty years, in connection with circumstances and incidents of very recent date, I am induced to hope and believe that this charge of fraud against Mrs. Cash has not been made with your knowledge or approval.

Please, Colonel, say if you made the charge, or if you have advised or encouraged any one else to do so. Very respectfully,   E. B. C. CASH.

To this letter Col. Shannon replied as follows:

CAMDEN, S. C., November 25, 1879.

Gen. E. B. C. Cash, Cash's Depot:

Dear General—Your kindly and courteous note is just received, and, amid pressing engagements, I reply at once, without consultation with any one.

I reciprocate fully the appreciation you express of "kindly relations that have existed between us for more than twenty years" (you might have said thirty-five,) and although I do not know what the "circumstances and incidents of very recent date" you refer to in the same spirit may be, I yet know there has been no change in those relations, so far as I am informed. And your "hope and belief" are reasonable that no charge whatever of "fraud," in any offensive sense, was made or intended, either by me or any other counsel in the cause, so far as I know.

In both cases I was only assistant counsel, and it was only courtesy toward me that induced the regular attorney in the causes to use my name as the leading counsel. He prepared the papers, and I only examined the witnesses and made an argument, in the first cause, all of which you saw or heard.

In the present suit I never read the papers at all. They were read to me just before they were filed, but I saw no marginal note, and knew nothing of either the margin being there or of its being erased; nor did I have anything to do with the erasure of the copy served on Mrs. Cash's attorney, knowing nothing of it one way or the other; but the erasure shows that the counsel who erased it withdrew it. I neither made it (and, of course) nor withdrew it.

I knew, of course, that, as counsel and an individual, I would be responsible for anything I assented to in the papers, and surely I would not shirk it if I were. But I neither knew of the existence nor withdrawal of the marginal clause. Don't know when it was put there or erased. But the copy shows it was withdrawn by whoever put it there, for the copy served is the authorized copy.

I am sure that I am confident that the regular attorney said, and meant to say nothing that could be regarded as a charge of fraud, in the sense you deem it as applicable. I know I never was rude to a lady in all these long years.

I know nothing whatever of the rights Mrs. Cash has in the property of Robert G. Ellerbe—whether her claims can be established or not. If they fail to be established, it would be because the law would hold that such a preference, as was thus made by the confession itself, is irregular, to one creditor over another, would work a legal fraud, not a fraud as you construe it; and I judge that was all the draughtsman of the complaint intended. That is matter of law and fact to be determined by the evidence, and is in no way offensive.

I hope you will find that this answer is as frank and kindly and satisfactory as you expected.   Very truly yours,   WM. M. SHANNON.

To this letter, Col. Cash replied:

CASH'S DEPOT, S. C., December 1, 1879.

Col. Wm. M. Shannon, Camden, S. C. :

Colonel—Your letter does not require a reply, but I wish to say it is substantially what I "hoped and believed" you would write me. I feel greatly relieved, for I have had no desire at any time to have a rupture with you. It is true, I felt very indignant at what appeared to be your course toward Mrs. Cash, and I sent a challenge to be delivered to you at Columbia, Fair week, or at Camden on the following Saturday. Hagood wisely and prudently stopped the delivery of the challenge, and when I went to Camden on the 17th, persons mutually friendly to us expressed their belief that the imputations cast upon Mrs. Cash's character had been made without your knowledge or approval. It was then that I thought of "incidents of recent date" that appeared inconsistent with a want of proper respect on your part for me, and I determined to write you my letter. In sending you the challenge I acted from a sense of duty to myself and my family, and from no desire to injure you, and I am truly happy to know there is no cause for any change of the friendly relations that have existed between us for many years.

Truly yours, E. B. C. CASH.

I desire now to invite the reader's attention to how, early in the correspondence, Col. Cash begins to thrust Mrs. Cash forward, that he may dodge behind her—that, while pretending to defend her honor, he was secretly seeking an excuse for the commission of the crime which he had in contemplation. Note, "Persons mutually friendly to us expressed their belief that "the imputations cast upon Mrs. Cash's character have been "made without your knowledge or approval."

I beg the reader to bear in mind that the reputed "imputation cast upon Mrs. Cash" was due to Col. Cash's own acts, as he acted for her without her knowledge. If there was an imputation cast upon Mrs. Cash's character, Col. Cash and Robert G. Ellerbe alone were responsible for it, and the pretence of vindicating her wounded name was but a subterfuge, intended to divert the public mind and to afford an excuse for the execution of the design which Col. Cash had upon the the lives of the attorneys who indicated the fraud of which he and Robert G. Ellerbe were guilty.

Col. Shannon's letter had silenced Col. Cash for a time, and he saw another pretext would have to be invented before he could proceed further with his murderous design.

On the 7th of February, 1880, Col. Cash attended Court at Camden, and in his pamphlet he says, alluding to Col. Shannon: "We met as friends, and nothing occurred in the investigation of the case to cause the slightest unkind feeling on my part to him, and I parted with him, without animosity or lack of friendship."

The reader will please observe the above statement. On the same page of his pamphlet Col. Cash says: "Col. Shannon examined the witnesses, and on leaving Camden I rode with Captain Ellerbe, who repeated to me some of the question asked him by Col. Shannon. I was not in court while Captain Ellerbe was on the stand, but from his report of the character of the examination, I felt assured that an effort had been made to create an impression that the transaction between Captain Ellerbe and his sister was fictitious, and I felt greatly provoked."

An excuse for seeking a meeting with either Col. Shannon or Captain DePass was now beginning to develop itself.

Admitting that Col. Shannon, in his examination of the

witnesses, asked certain questions, the effect of which was to create an impression that the transaction between Robert G. Ellerbe and Col. Cash was fictitious, what does it prove? Does it show any inconsistency, when compared with Col. Shannon's letter to Col. Cash? Not at all. Let us see. In his letter Col. Shannon says:

> In the present suit I never read the papers at all. They were read to me just before they were filed, but I saw no marginal note, and I knew nothing of either the margin being there or of its being erased: nor did I have anything to do with the erasure on the copy served on Mrs. Cash's attorney; knowing nothing of it one way or another; but the erasure shows that the counsel who erased it withdrew it. I neither erased it (and of course) nor withdrew it. * * I know nothing whatever of the rights Mrs. Cash has in the property of Robert G. Ellerbe—whether her claims can be established or not."

The reader will remember that the marginal note, which gave offence to Col. Cash, was not the work of Col. Shannon, and he will bear in mind also that the letter from which the above extract is made, disclaiming any charge of fraud, was written more than two months before the session of the court, at which Col. Shannon's questions to witnesses implied that the arrangement between Robert G. Ellerbe and Col. Cash was fictitious.

It is quite easy to reconcile these two points. When Col. Shannon's letter was written, November 25, 1879, he was only partially informed, and "knew nothing whatever of the rights " of Mrs. Cash in the property of Robert G. Ellerbe." Before the next term of the court, however, he investigated the matter and assured himself that the reputed confession of judgment was fictitious; hence the questions which he is reputed to have asked witnesses, and charges made.

> Charges of fraud were distinctly, repeatedly, and expressly made. * * Col. Shannon was the leading counsel for the plaintiff, and examined all the witnesses; and surely ought to have known the positions he wished to establish. Reader, please bear in mind that all this occurred after the attention of Col. Shannon had been called to the matter in November."

True, perhaps, and if so, what of it? Certain, it appears, that we no more see Col. Shannon denying the charges of which Col. Cash complained. He was convinced that there had been fraud, and could not afford to be silent on that point, merely because Col. Cash had called his attention to the matter in the month of November peceding.

Now, reader, here is the situation: Col. Cash and Robert G. Ellerbe had entered into a "family arrangement" for the purpose of defeating recovery by Weinges. They had used the name of Mrs. Cash to that end without consulting her. In the complaint this charge was made in a marginal note by W. L. DePass. Col. Cash wrote to Col. Shannon, calling his attention to the marginal note. Col. Shannon replies that he knows nothing about it, and declares his ignorance upon other points. Later, he sees that the charges set forth in the summons and complaint are substantially true, authough, in the authorized copy, the offensive clause is omitted. At the next term of court the questions which he asks witnesses are understood as being put to create the impression that the arrangement entered into between Robert G. Ellerbe and Col. Cash, wherein they employ the name of Mrs. Cash without her knowledge or consent, is fictitious.

This is deemed a deadly offence, and Col. Cash declares: "I could no longer be in doubt; I felt I had no recourse but to "hold these lawyers responsible for the imputations cast upon "Mrs. Cash."

Had Col. Cash desired to vindicate his wife, instead of wreaking vengeance upon the heads of Messrs. Shannon and DePass, why did he not come out and say that he and Robert G. Ellerbe alone were responsible for the transaction, and that his wife had no part in it. Why did he not testify then as he has since testified under oath, "Witness had no personal in-"terest in the claim of Mrs. Cash against Robert G. Ellerbe, "and did not consult with Mrs. Cash."

That would have more effectually exonerated Mrs. Cash in the eyes of the world than would have been possible by any resort to arms. That would have shifted the responsibility to the shoulders which should have borne it, and the world would long since have understood that which, at this late day, it becomes my part to make plain, viz: That Col. Cash and his brother-in-law, Robert G. Ellerbe, perpetrated a fraud, shifted the blame to Mrs. Cash, and then murdered an innocent man to conceal their iniquity, under pretense of redressing Mrs. Cash's wrongs. In self-extenuation he says:

"On the 12th day of April, I was taken seriously sick, and while Mrs. Cash was showing me every kind attention, on the 14th she was stricken speechless, and lingered and died on the 19th of April. She was a proud, high-spirited, noble Christian. I do not believe the fear of death could have influenced her to deviate from the strictest truth, but, in the interest of peace, and to prevent the effusion of blood, she concealed her sorrows from me, and to my promise to punish her assailants, she replied, 'O, no, I can live above such imputations.' After she died, I learned that she had been sorely annoyed by the charges of infamy against her spotless character, and I resolved to revenge her wrongs or forfeit my life in the effort to do so."

It is Col. Cash's purpose, in the above, to create the impression that Mrs. Cash's death was occasioned, or hastened, by by the imputations above indicated.

Such is indeed possible, and it is even highly probable that the charges had much to do with hastening her end. Poor lady! It was truly enough to crush her, when she came to understand how her brother and the husband of her youth had entered into a fraudulent combination, using her name without consulting her, and thus bringing unmerited adium down upon her! Alas! poor lady, not Col. Cash, but she it was who—

"Had wrongs to stir the blood of age!"

She sank beneath her wrongs—sank beneath the blow a husband and a brother had dealt. So far from desiring to murder some one else, it rather seems that Col. Cash should have preferred destroying himself.

He "resolved to revenge her wrongs or forfeit his life in the effort to do so." Gracious! Think, reader, think of this chivalric devotion! and then think of the time when the poor invalid wife and mother was carried to her girlhood's home on a mattress and rudely deposited on the floor. Think of the man who feared to face the invalid's brothers and who concealed himself in the bushes, awaiting for those brothers to leave, so that he might enter their home and bully their sister. Think of how he entered that home and robbed the poor invalid of her baby boy—her first born. Think of how she follows him, against her inclination. Think of her sufferings, for many a weary year, till, unable to endure her wrongs longer, she was compelled a second time to separate from her husband, and again seek an asylum with her mother. Think of how her little girl was stolen from her in Camden. Think of her forced return to the home in which she had suffered so much. Think of the presence of her husband's hybrid children scattered all over the plantation. Think of the presence of her husband's mulatto mistress, under the same roof with herself. Think of this mistress' being her husband's own child by a negress. Think of her baby whom her husband stole from her in infancy, grown to be a man, and rising up in righteous indignation, to rebuke his father for his sickening sins. Think of her husband's drawing his pistol to shoot her boy, because he had dared to raise his voice and protest against her wrongs. Think of this boy, a few years later, becoming so imbruted, that he rivals his incestuous father in the lust of his mistress, and himself becomes guilty of incest with his mulatto sister, Juliana. Think of the frequent and oft-repeated brawls between father and son, on account of this wretch. Think of the arrangement entered into between husband and brother, in which her name was used without her consent, and of the odium which attached to her name in consequence. Think of these things, reader, and then ask yourself the question: What does Col. Cash mean by saying, he "resolved to revenge his wife's wrongs or die in the effort to do so?"

No, reader, Col. Cash's object was not to vindicate his wife's honor. Neither was his purpose to redress her wrongs, for the only wrongs which she had suffered, she suffered at the hands of her husband and her brother, Robert G. Ellerbe. The secret of the matter is, Col. Cash had been thwarted, temporarily, at least, and he thirsted for revenge—he panted for blood, and blood he was determined to have.

About the 20th of May, 1880, or one month after the death of Mrs. Cash, Col. Cash went to the residence of his brother-in-law, Robert G. Ellerbe, near Camden, S. C. Two days later,

Robert G. Ellerbe sent a challenge to Col. Shannon, and Col. Cash sent a Challenge to W. L. DePass. Captain DePass accepted Col. Cash's challenge, and it was agreed that they should meet at DuBois' Bridge, Darlington county, S. C., 1880. Several days before the time appointed for the meeting, DePass was arrested and placed under bond. I have always believed that Captain DePass did not intend to fight, and that his acceptance of the challenge was but a hoax. I have always believed he had nither the moral courage to decline the challenge nor the physical courage to fulfill the engagement after having made it. There never were two men yet, both desiring to fight, who could not find a time and a place for the execution of their insane desire. ("Whom the Gods would destroy they first make mad.")

Col. Shannon very promptly declined to meet Robert G. Ellerbe. No definite reason was assigned for this refusal, but it was understood that, even if Ellerbe had been justifiable in sending the challeng, Col. Shannon would have been inexcusable in accepting it—inexcusable in meeting on an equality a man of Robert G. Ellerbe's stamp.

Of course he declined, for what gentleman, respecring himself, could stoop to the level of Robert G. Ellerbe. Not Col. William M. Shannon, truly.

For refusing to meet Ellerbe, Prof. Carlisle, of Spartanburg, S. C., wrote Col. Shannon, commending his action, but the Doctor was much chagrinned when Col. Shannon replied that, under certain circumstances, he would fight a duel, but that, aside from Ellerbe's lack of excuse in challenging him, he could not afford to meet a man of Robert G. Ellerbe's social standing.

Ellerbe knew beforehand that Col. Shannon could not and would not accept his challenge, but when it was declined, he "posted" Col. Shannon in the following filthy and disgusting card:

BOYKIN'S DEPOT, S. C., May 24th, 1880.

William M. Shannon, Esq., Camden, S, C.:

Sir—Your note of this date has been handed me by your friend, Mr. Wm. E. Johnson, by which said note you deny my right to call you to account for any statements made in certain proceedings in court, though you insist that you shirk no responsibility. You also deny my right to call you to the Field of Honor on any accouut, and decline my invitation to fight. I was under the imdression, from your letters to Col. Cash, that you would shirk no responsibility, but I find I am mistaken—that you are one of those unenvioble men who insult gentlemen and then refuse to aceount to them the usual satisfaction which brave men award to those who consider themselves aggrieved. Your refusal to fight leaves me no alternative than to denounce you as a paltroon and a coward, and to hold you up as an object of contempt to all brave men. R. G, ELLERBE.

It is not to be supposed for one moment that this document ruffled in any degree the serene and even-tempered Shannon. He felt too sensibly the gulf which nature, circumstance and education had placed between Robert G. Ellerbe and himself, to feel at all aggrieved at anything that individual might say or think concerning himself. In his letter to Robert G. Ellerbe, declining the challenge, Col. Shannon said: "Your language, intended to be offensive, makes no impression on me, nor will it on any one who may happen to know us both." This declaration, of course, applied with equal force to to Ellerbe's card, and no self-respecting gentleman could blame him for ignoring it.

On the 27th of May, 1880, Captain DePass offered to go beyond the South Carolina limits and fight Col. Cash, and it was agreed that they should meet at a point in Anson county, N. C. Captain DePass, (at his own instance, I think,) was again arrested. Captain W. L. R. Blair, Captain DePass's second, waited upon Col. Cash and notified him of Captain DePass' arrest, whereupon Col. Cash grew furious and denounced Capt. DePass in the most violent terms. Captain Blair, however, was not only a man of undoubted courage, but he was also desperately rash, and was willing to fight Col. Cash or anybody else, any way and at any time and place. He was especially desirous of taking a pop at Col. Cash with a double-barrel gun loaded with buck-shot. Col. Cash knew this, but he was not at all disposed to accommodate Captain Blair. Therefore it is not strange that when Captain Blair interrupted Col. Cash in his denunciation of Capt. DePass with the remark: "Colonel, though it is true that DePass cannot fulfill his engagement, yet there is no reason why the programme should not be acted out to the end. Colonel, I am here, and I stand in Captain DePass' place. Col. Cash, Captain DePass' friend is at your service!"—therefore, I say, it is not strange that to this remark Col. Cash should have replied, "Blair, I have no quarrel with you. Come, let us take a drink."

A few days after this, Col. Cash published the correspondpondence and "posted" DePass.

The citizens of Camden, by this time, were worked up to a fever heat, and they organized what was known as the "Camden Anti-Dueling Society," the objects of which were indicated by its name. A few days after its organization, Col. Cash wrote a severe article denouncing the Society and Messrs. Shannon DePass, but without calling the names of said gentlemen. The article was first published in the Carolina Sun, (Col. Cash's county paper,) and was extensively copied. I give it below:

Cash's Depot, S. C., June 8, 1880.

I have seen the News and Courier of this date, containing a report of the proceedings of a body of men in Camden, who style themselves "An Anti-Dueling Association," and have also observed the editorial remarks on the same subject. As my name is closely associated with these movements, I desire to notice them, but feel confident that were I to apply for the use of the columns of the News and Courier, I would meet with refusal. I, therefore, beg you for the use of your paper, hoping that other papers in the State may copy what I have to say. No one will doubt that the editors of the News and Courier are in full sympathy with the anti-dueling movement their past records and private characters are such as not only to qualify them for full membership to such an association, but would justify their elevation to prominent positions in the same. We are informed that this Camden Association is composed of men who will do their whole duty, and put an end to the "criminal" practice of dueling.

Camden has grown pious very slow, very! As long as her men would fight we heard not one word about the "criminal practice of dueling." For years that section has been regarded as the Galway of the State, and only a short time ago Williams and Cantey were permitted to leave the town to fight duels; there was no howling on those occasions. Williams and Cantey were willing to fight and were not molested; but just as soon as two of the leading citizens of the town strike their colors and take to their heels (in order to divert attention and hide their tracks), up pops an anti-dueling society with a reformed drunkard, the tail end of the bench, as president, and I suppose with every braggart and bully in town as members. Such an association will be a bomb-proof and a God-send to all the liars, slanderers and cowards of the place. They can speak of their neighbors as they please, and when called to account will "shirk" their responsibility by pleading membership of this association.

What a pity this movement had not been inaugurated two weeks ago! It would have served as a coat of mail for an intimate friend and close connection of the pious president, and saved a vast amount of white-washing, rendered necessary by recent events. These archangels take it upon themselves to denounce as "criminal" the acts of men who are as far their superiors as the eagle is the superior of the buzzard. These poor creatures denounce as "criminals" such men as Andrew Jackson, Henry Clay, John Rutledge, Alexander Hamilton, John Laurens, Commodore Perry, and thousands of others of the best and purest men who inhabit the civilized portion of the world. In their agony, and for the present occasion, they would denounce as criminals our own Perry, and Gist, and McDuffie, and Dunnovant, and Rhett, and Taber and Magarth.

Will this army corps of seraphs and cherubs tell us poor deluded creatures what they propose as a substitute for the duel? Will they be kind enough to suggest some better and more humane plan by which the weak can be put upon a footing with the strong? Will they tell us how the pigmy is to meet the giant? Or are they such fools as to think that the Millennium is at hand, or that from the date of their first meeting all strife and contention will cease throughout the world? Respectfully, E. B. C. CASH.

Following quick upon the publication of the above letter came that villainous lampoon, "Camden Soliloquies," written, as Boggan Cash himself declares, for the express purpose of exasperating Col. Shannon to a fight. This vile effusion is below given:

CAMDEN SOLILOQUIES.

Now ain't this shameful! DePass is to blame for it all. He said he could stir up old Weinges to sue Ellerbe, and we would make a fat thing of it. Well, he has played the devil. No money up to date and prospects growing dim, and I have had to take water like a dog. I knew I would not fight, but I did not want others to know it. They say blood will tell, and I believe it is true. My daddy was a gin-maker and I don't think people ought to expect to me fight; but I have tried to make them believe I would. It is over with me now and I am " Bully Billy" no longer. I wish I had never heard of the case, and, oh God, if I could only recall the letters I wrote to that old devil, Cash; but I know he has got them and will show them. I made him believe I was game, but gave him no chance to try me. I want nothing to do with the old wretch. They say he kills people and then eats them up, and I believe he meant to eat up DePass, if he could have found him.

It may be I am not such bad blood after all. I am sometimes afraid that it is my own meanness that makes me weak. I let my daring boy risk his life for me and then this bridge business is a sore to me. I am afraid the people don't know how honest I am. Then I have cheated widows and orphans and my own sister out of all she had—took her toy clock and put it up to the highest bidder; but after all a fellow must live, and is worse than an infidel if he don't provide for his own family. I shall now join old Wilson's Anti-Dueling Society, and I think I ought to be first president.

> My daddy was a gin-maker—
> And worked cheek by jowl,
> With Ellison, a negro,
> ('Tis a secret,) by my soul.
>
> My daddy was a gin-maker—
> And worked on old saws.
> I am stealing Billy,
> An expounder of the laws.
>
> My daddy was a gin-maker,
> A damned old fool was he;
> I made my money,
> By bridging the Wateree.
>
> My daddy was a gin-maker,
> Damn such an occupation;
> I can live by swindling,
> And on my reputation.
>
> My daddy was a gin-maker—
> No fighting man was he—
> And as long as I have legs to run,
> No man shall shoot at me.

Compliments of   W. B. CASH.

In his pamphlet Col. Cash lays particular stress upon the fact that he met Col. Shannon at the solicitation of that gentleman, for the "purpose of settling a personal difficulty that had arisen between them," and he repudiates the charge of "hounding down his victim" and availing himself of a "long-sought opportunity." The reader of the foregoing pages can judge for himself how much truth there is in Col. Cash's denial of these charges, and when it is borne in mind that the "Camden Soliloquies" were published upon the back of R. G. Ellerbe's circular containing the correspondence between himself and Col. Shannon and his denunciation of that gentleman, it cannot be questioned that Col. Cash wilfully falsifies when he denies that between himself, Robert G. Ellerbe and W. B. Cash, Col. Shannon was goaded on to a point of desperation when it became absolutely necessary for him to do something. He felt that was a duty he owed to his family to kill Col. Cash or die himself, but it is possible the consciousness of his innocence, his sense of infinite superiority to his maligners, would have deterred him from taking any action in the matter, but for the fact that his son, Mr. William M. Shannon, Jr., was about to act himself, and this Col. Shannon could not permit. Therefore, on the 11th June, 1880, Col. Shannon addressed to following letter to Col. Cash:

CAMDEN, S. C., June 11th, 1880.

Gen. E. B. C. Cash, Cash's Depot, S. C.:

Sir—In the correspondence between us from the 24th of November to the 1st of December, 1879, and in subsequent personal interviews, you expressed yourself as gratified and satisfied at the solution of all matters involved, and yet, on the 20th of May, 1880, in relation to the said matters, in your presence and surely with your approval, Mr. R. G. Ellerbe addresses me a coarse, false and insulting letter based upon that correspondence, and the matters it referred to, and containing a "demand for redress and a hostile meeting." For reasons satisfactory to myself I decline to accede to that demand, and with that correspondence I rest content.

Yesterday there was shown me a circular containing that correspondence endorsed by your son, W. B. Cash, in scurrilous, vulgar, libelous, false and dirty language, in which the correspondence between you and me is referred to and threats issued as to what you will do with it, and you are held up as an ogre and a cannible to "fright me from my propriety."

I have no issue with Mr. W. B. Cash, and the style and matter of that endorsement forbid my directly noticing that endorsement, but as all these things result from a present dissatisfaction with the correspondence between you and me, and as there has been no change in the condition of affairs since then, I ask to call your attention to the fact, that I held myself responsible in that correspondence for all that I had done, and I now add that I hold myself responsible to you for all the false positions you and yours have seen fit to assign me.

Without investigation you have seen fit to place me there, and I see no reason for adjourning to others a difficulty which your inaugurated

Motives of convenience and privacy both induce me to forward this by mail. Respectfully, WM. M. SHANNON.

To this letter Col. Cash replied in the following obnoxious and disgusting terms:

CASH'S DEPOT, S. C., June 15, 1880.

Col. W. M. Shannon :

Sir—Yours of the 11th came to hand last night. In reply I have to say that I have with great reluctance come to the settled conclusion that you are the unmitigated scoundrel you have been represented to be by those who have known you better than I did. When I called upon you in November for an explanation of your conduct toward Mrs. Cash, you expressed entire ignorance of the charge against her character, and most emphatically disavowed any intention of being offensive, and your deceitful and treacherous behavior to me on the day the injunction was served on your sheriff aided you in deceiving me, and inducing me to believe your false professions were sincere and true, and I was truly gratified to know there was to be no trouble between us, and I wrote a candid and honest letter, expressing my pleasure that we were to remain friendly. But, sir, I have since learned that your assertions were basely false, and that you were acting the part of a hypocrite to avoid your responsibility to me. After disclaiming in the most positive manner any intention to charge Mrs. Cash with fraud, you went into court and did all in your power to establish a case of fraud against her. I was in court but a short part of the time while Mr. Ellerbe was on the witness stand, and could hear but little while I was present, but he has reported to me some of the questions you asked him, which show beyond all doubt that you hoped to be able to prove a charge of fraud. This, sir, was after you had denied to me that you had made a charge of fraud. But sir, to rivet and clinch falsehood upon you, I call your attention to the decision of the presiding judge. If you made no charge of fraud, how could he decide that neither Mrs. Cash nor her brother were guilty of fraud? You cannot get around this matter by putting it off on the junior counsel in the case. Your attention had been called to the matter before the trial, and if you and he could not agree upon the manner in which the case was to be conducted, it was your duty, if you had been honest, to have withdrawn from the management of the case, and any one with a spark of principle in his character would surely have done so.

When I heard the nature of the questions you propounded to Mr. Ellerbe, and the decision the judge had made, I became convinced that you had lied to me, and it was my purpose to have called on you for a settlement as soon as circumstances would have made it safe for me to proceed against you; but your refusal to fight Mr. Ellerbe, and the fact that you have been advertised as a paltroon and a coward by a man who is your superior by birth and in all the essentials and characteristics that constitute an honcrable man, places you beyond the recognition of those who wish to be regarded as gentlemen. The position has been assumed by some that a gentleman may, if challenged, fight his boot black, and the good opinion I once had of you, and the inborn sympathy I possess for those in distress, prompts me to adopt (for the present) that position towards you, and I think I have given you in this note ample and sufficient grounds to justify you in taking action against me, and should you determine to act on my suggestion, allow me to assure you that no friend of mine will meanly resort to the law to punish you for sending me a challenge. Nor will I attempt to array public opinion against you by claiming that you have placed me in a false position. E. B. C. CASH.

Those who have only read Col. Cash's version of his trouble may think that he was wronged by Col. Shannon, but those who know the facts on both sides, know such to be untrue, and only a few dexterous strokes of the pen are necessary to render the above letter ridiculous.

1st. He states his settled conviction that Col. Shannon is an "unmitigated scoundrel." Note.—In his pamphlet, written many months after the date of the above letter, he speaks of Col. Shannon as a genial, cultivated gentlemen, with whom, for more than twenty five years it had been his pleasure to meet. Will Col. Cash, can Col. Cash, reconcile these difference to the satisfaction of the public mind?

2nd. Col. Shannon's professed ignorance of a charge of fraud, etc. I have already shown on page 45 how there was no inconsistency between Col. Shannon's letter to Col. Cash, disclaiming all intention of making a charge of fraud and his subsequent action in court. It is there made plain that Col. Shannon did nothing amiss, and that his conduct toward Col. Cash was neither deceitful, hypocritical nor treacherous.

3rd. Col. Shannon "advertised as a paltroon and a coward by a man who was his superior by birth and in all the essentials and characteristics that constitute an honorable man," etc. Without pausing here to analyze the character of the rough, the rowdy, the drunkard, Robert G. Ellerbe, whom Col. Cash regarded as the superior of Col. Shannon in all the "essentials and characteristics that constitute an honorable man," I will only cite the reader's attention to Chapter IV, and he can see for himself how superior to Col. Shannon was this sweet-scented creature, Robert G. Ellerbe, by birth, as well as in "all the essentials and characteristics that constitute an honorable man." And right here I would like to see Col. Cash arise and explain to the world what relation this Robert G. Ellerbe sustains to Thomas Ellerbe, who murdered a North Carolina wagoner and fled to Florida, where he murdered his own son; also to Boggan Ellerbe, who once came to Wadesboro with the intention of murdering his uncle; also to Dr. W. C. Ellerbe, before more mentioned; also to Zack Ellerbe, who stabbed his own son to death with a knife, and afterwards shot a little negro boy, for which he was sent to the penitentiary; also to the sons of Zach Ellerbe, three of whom did one Sunday morning hem a bull in a pen and beat the poor animal to death with their fists; also if this Robert G. Ellerbe is not the same Robert G. Ellerbe who used the interest of his sister in her father's estate for a period of thirty-one years, without paying in all more than $500 for the use of the same; also if he is not the same Robert G. Ellerbe who "held the lands, stock and all other property of his mother, Mrs. E. M. Ellerbe, in his possession during the entire period, and used and enjoyed the proceeds and profits arising therefrom WITHOUT EVER PAYING ANYTHING FOR IT." Verily this Robert G. Ellerbe must be a superior man by birth and in "all the essentials and characteristics that constitute an honorable man!"

4th. Couldn't afford to challenge Col. Shannon but would accept a challenge. There is more in this than the casual reader might think at first glance. It was not that Col. Cash really deemed Col. Shannon beneath his recognition after he had been posted by the honorable Robert G. Ellerbe, but because Col. Cash had an inkling that Col. Shannon, if he had the choice of weapons, would select double-barrel guns loaded with buckshot,— and that is an agent of destruction which Col. Cash can't face, as has been successfully demonstrated on more than one occasion.

Accompanying the above letter was the following effusion from W. B. Cash:

CASH'S DEPOT, S. C., June 15, 1880.

Col. W. M. Shannon:

Sir—I have seen your letter to my father. I am truly gratified to know the medicine I administered to you is having such happy effect. I placed it where I thought it would do most good, but from fear of failure sent you a notice of what course I was pursuing. You, sir, meanly and basely slandered my mother and my uncle with the hope of filling your empty pockets. When called to account by my father you deceived him by the most unblushing falsehoods, which he is now prepared to prove upon you to the satisfaction of any intelligent and disinterested man. When my uncle demanded satisfaction from you for the injury you had done him, you took water like a dog, although you had previously claimed you would shirk no responsibility. You now write my father and intimate that you are willing to answer for the wrongs that you have done, but at the same time time you beg the question by saying he "has placed you in a false position." But apart from that you know he could not challenge you without going back on my uncle, who had branded you as a paltroon and a coward. You felt that you were in a bomb-proof, and there you intend to remain as long as you live. Aside from your recent disgraceful conduct, the great disparity of our ages prevents my going upon you; but if there is any of your blood who would like to espouse your infamous cause, I am ready and will gladly meet them at any time and place that will be mutually convenient. W. B. CASH.

There was not the shadow of an excuse for the above letter. After reading "Camden Soliloquies," Col. Shannon declared he had no issue with W. B. Cash and could not ntice his scurrilous effusion. The above letter was written, it must appear evident, with the sole view of provoking Col. Shannon into challenging Col. Cash, should the latter's vile letter of June 13, 1880, fail in doing so.

I have said before that Col. Cash denies "hounding down his victim." The facts and the correspondence are now before the reader—let him decide for himself.

I have met and refuted, I think, every point which Col. Cash has made, or endeavored to make, in his pamphlet, in self-extenuation. There is one statement, however, which he makes, and which it surprises me he should make, that I have not yet noticed. Says Col. Cash: "My son W. B. Cash wrote what he " styled 'Camden Soliloquies,' in a spirit of retaliation, and as " the only means available of resenting the wrongs inflicted up- " his mother. I am sure the idea never occurred to him that " what he did could lead to any meeting between Col. Shan- " non and myself. * * Nor do I believe the article written by " my son had aught to do in producing the fight between Col. " Shannon and myself."

I am now compelled to charge Col. Cash with knowingly, wilfully falsifying. He knew he was telling an untruth when he made the above statement, and it is surprising that he should have been so blind as not to see every one could detect his falsehood when he gave publicity to the foregoing letter of W. B. Cash, wherein it is explicitly stated that he was "gratified to " know that the medicine he administered was having such " happy effect * * but from fear of failure, sent notice of what " course he was pursuing."

Unable longer to endure the Cashes' persecution, Col. Shannon addressed the following note to Col. Cash:

CAMDEN, S. C., June 27, 1880.

SIR: Your letter of the 15th was duly received. In reply to its insulting contents I have to demand of you that redress which is usual under such circumstances. My friend, Mr. W. E. Johnson, will make all necessary arrangements for a hostile meeting. Respectfully, WM. M. SHANNON.

To this letter Col. Cash promptly responded, and in fancy I can see him gloating with fiendish rapture over the prospect of the impending meeting as he pens the following lines:

CASH'S DEPOT, S. C., June 28, 1880.

Col. W. M. Shannon, Camden, S. C.:

Your note of the 27th has been handed me by your friend, Mr. W. E. Johnson, and my friend, ———— has arranged with Mr. Johnson for a meeting between us, when I hope to be able to accord you the redress you demand. Respectfully, E. B. C. CASH.

It was agreed between Mr. W. E. Johnson and W. B. Cash that Col. Shannon and Col. Cash should meet at the highland above DuBois' Bridge, in Darlington county, S. C., between the hours of 1 and 3 o'clock, on Monday the 5th day of July, 1880. It was agreed that the combatants should stand at fifteen paces distant, and that the "second winning the word should raise "his pistol and ask, 'are you ready?' and then discharge the "pistol in the air, and the parties may fire after such discharge "but not after the word halt!"

The point of meeting was about midway between Camden and the residence of Col. Cash. Col. Shannon was the first to arrive upon the ground with his party, and very soon thereafter Col. Cash drove up, accompanied by Mr. W. B. Saunders, his second, and W. B. Cash and Robert G. Ellerbe.

It was generally known, for quite twenty-four hours beforehand, that the duel would take place, and about two hundred persons from the surrounding country had congregated to witness the encounter, but there was no officer of the law present to prevent it.

Mr. Saunders stepped off the distance, and the principals were placed in position, after which they bade adieu to their friends and seconds. Mr. Johnson was stationed on the right of Col. Shannon in his rear, and Mr. Saunders on the left, opposite Mr. Johnson.

Mr. Johnson won the word and directed the firing. At "one," Col. Shannon fired; a moment after, at "two," Col. Cash fired. Col. Shannon stood erect for an instant, then stepped once forward, staggered to the right and fell. The surgeons in attendance hastened to him, and found, upon examination, that the ball had entered the right breast, near the nipple, passed into the body, and ranged about two inches above the heart (not through the heart, as has been stated). Death was almost instantaneous, painless and with scarce a struggle. Thus came untimely to his end this brave and tender man, at the hands of a trio of ruffians, one of whom has already met with a deserved fate, and it is to be hoped that the remaining two, sooner or later, will find themselves in the grasp of retributive justice.

In his pamphlet Col. Cash says: "The fight was fair and "equal, and there has been no complaint on the part of his "his friends that I sought or obtained any advantage over "him."

Col. Cash if right. There has been no complaint on the part of Col. Shannon's friends. Whatever they may think or feel is forever hid from the world, and their lips are forever sealed against the Cashes. True, there has been no complaint from that source, but there are others, Col. Cash, who are not compelled to abide the result of that duel. The charge HAS BEEN made that the fight WAS NOT "fair and equal," and if certain information which I have received during the last few months could be proven true, Col. Cash ought yet to be taken up and hanged higher than Haman!

Col. WM. M. SHANNON,
Killed in a duel by Col. E. B. C. Cash, July 5, 1880.

It has long been whispered, with bated breath, in Marlboro and Chesterfield counties, that Col. Cash wears a metalic shield beneath his clothing. I know not what reason the people of Chesterfield and Marlboro have for this intimation, but I do know what reason I have for believing that the intimation may be true: After Boggan Cash shot the Marshal of Cheraw, a negro boy who had been with the Cashes for years, through fear of being killed himself, ran away from them and came to Wadesboro. While here he told a colored man now in my employ—and in whose veracity I have full confidence—of Cash's metalic shield. From the description which he gave of the shield, I am forced to believe there must be some truth in the statement, for that ignorant boy could not have imagined and so accurately described such a contrivance, unless he had seen something of the kind.

The tale that Col. Shannon's ball struck the ground in a line with Col. Cash's body and threw sand in his face is very improbable. Will the reader pause a moment and consider what an improbable tale that is.

Since I have given my attention to the particulars of this duel, I have tried the experiment of shooting, as Col. Shannon is reputed to have shot, fully one hundred times, and every shot has convinced me that, in the report of the duel, there has been a mistake somewhere.

Col. Cash admits that he did not know where Col. Shannon's ball had gone, until he was informed by his friend, Mr. A. H. Warren, after leaving the field, that it had struck the ground near him. The spectators were standing from 100 to 500 yards from the combatants; how then could Mr. Waring see where the ball had gone? The seconds had their eyes riveted on their principals; how could they see where the ball went?

Col. Shannon was a brave man; he was an accurate shot; when within two miles of the dueling ground he alighted from his buggy and practiced at a target; his aim was then faultless; when placed in position he was perfectly cool and self-possessed. How then could it be possible for his ball to go in the ground fifteen feet from Col. Cash?

Reader, it never did it. At the word "one," the ball from Col. Shannon's pistol went unerringly to Col. Cash's breast, but its course was arrested by that metalic shield. It rebounded fifteen feet, and it was thus that it left its mark on the ground fifteen feet from Cash's body.

This is I believe it true. I believe Col. Cash wears a bullet proof shield over the vital parts of his cowardly person Indeed, so sure am I that he goes thus protected, that I would advise all persons should they ever have any trouble with Col. Cash, not to shoot at his body but to aim at his head. For my own part, if I ever have any trouble with him, I shall endeavor to pop him midway between the horns!

CHAPTER IX.

Stormy Lives of the Cashes for the Last Four Years.

"The mill of the Gods grinds slow, but grinds exceeding fine."

Col. Cash presented himself in Darlington, at the October term of the court for said county, in 1880, to be tried for "murder" and for "dueling." The case was continued, and a hearing was had some months afterwards, when a mis-trial was ordered. Again was Col. Cash put on trial June 21st, 1881. This time he was "honorably acquitted." No one expected his conviction. For more than a hundred years dueling had been connived at in South Carolina. It was regarded as the proper mode of settling personal affairs between gentlemen. No one had ever been punished in that State for fighting a duel, and no one expected Col. Cash to be punished.

However, though the courts were powerless to punish Col. Cash, yet were there two other tribunals before which he was arraigned—Public Sentiment and his own Guilty Conscience—and before both of these tribunals has he been convicted and punished. Since the tragic affair at DuBois' Bridge, Col. Cash has not been the same man that was before. Remorse for his crime, the condemnation of his fellow-men, the loss of human sympathy, all tend to render the old man wretched. Though he is to be heartily despised, yet is he truly a pitiable object.

It is sad to behold in that grey-headed old man the embodiment of all that is mean and vicious, and to realize the fact that he has wrought his own ruin—that he has blasted every hope which must once have cherished—that he has brought undying shame upon his name and his memory—all by licensing his evil passions to run riot and by denying to others the same rights which he claimed for himself.

Before the duel, the Cashes, father and son, were bad enough, but since then, and up to the time of Boggan's death, they have been intolerable. They have been in continuous turmoil and a series of the most disgusting broils has characterized their lives.

In 1882 Col. Cash was nominated by the Independent Greenback party for Congress in the 5th Congressional District of South Carolina. His canvass of the District was as ridiculous as disgraceful. I have been unable to learn of any incident which characterized it, worthy of mention here, unless, perchance, it be the row which he succeeded in inaugurating between the races at Lancaster C. H., in which the editor of the Lancaster Ledger and a number of white men were hurt and a dozen or so negroes killed.

Col. Cash was not elected, as is generally known, and from the day of his defeat, nothing is heard of him, outside of his own balewick, until the 23rd of February, 1884, when his son, W. B. Cash, shot and killed the Marshal of Cheraw, and Mr. James Coward, an unoffending bystander, with whom the Marshal was talking at the time he was shot.

The particulars of this tragedy, and the causes which led to it, have already been fully discussed in the first part of this sketch. Let us now return to the incidents set forth in Chapter I, and trace the life of Boggan from the 23rd of February, 1880, to the day of his tragic end, a few weeks thereafter.

When it was known in Cheraw that the Marshal had been shot, the wildest excitement prevailed. With electric rapidity the news spread through the town, and the throb of the popular pulse was, "Death to the assassin!"

After firing the third time, Cash ran for a hundred yards, brandishing his pistol to intimmidate pursuers and calling aloud to his boy to bring him his horse; but the boy, frightened out of his wits, was powerless to move, and Boggan was forced to retreat to where animal was standing. Mounting the spirited steed, he dashed away swift as the wind. There was some talk among the citizens of pursuing and apprehending the murderer, but no effort was made in that direction.

When the up train passed Cash's Depot, an hour later, Boggan was seen excitedly pacing to and fro in front of the Cash mansion, armed with a Winchester rifle, while his father stood passively by, making no demonstration. It is thought they were waiting see if there would come any one from Cheraw to arrest Boggan.

As soon as possible after the shooting, Sheriff Spofford, who lives at Chesterfield Court-House, some fifteen miles from Cheraw, was notified of what had happened. Armed with the necessary papers, and accompanied by one of his deputies, he next day repaired to residence of Col. Cash. The Sheriff and deputy were met at the door by the Colonel, who invited them in most cordially. He made them a brandy-smash and treated them most hospitably—so hospitably, indeed, that they came away without making the arrest, although Boggan must have been concealed somewhere about the premises.

The county authorities taking no action in the matter, and it appearing that nothing would be done by said authorities, the Governor of South Carolina, after having offered a reward of $500 for the apprehension of Boggan Cash, sent State Constable Richbourg, in charge of twelve picked men, to see what could be done.

Captain Richbourg and posse left Columbia at midnight,

March 8th, and at 3:30 o'clock, March 9th, took a special train at Florence for their destination. Arriving within a mile of Cash's Depot, the force disembarked and quietly proceeded up the railroad track on foot. Captain Richbourg stationed his men around the mansion and waited for daylight. Just as day began to dawn, Col. Cash went out on his back piazza to take his morning bitters, and there beheld the News and Courier's good-looking Gonzales standing a few yards away with a Springfield rifle in his hands and quietly surveying Col. Cash's actions. The old man hailed Gonzales, but no response coming, he instantly took in the situation and darted back into the house. Armed with a Winchester rifle, a Colt's revolver and the dueling pistol with which he killed Col. Shannon, he slipped out the front door and tried to make his way through the pickets to a house, a short distance away, wherein incestuous Boggan was passing the night with his mulatto sister Juliana. Col. Cash had not gone more than a hundred yards before he came suddenly upon J. H. Pearson, one of the sentinels, who covered the old man with his rifle and told him to drop his gun or that he would fall himself in two seconds. The gun was instantly dropped. Col. Cash threw up his hands, prayed for mercy and begged that his life be spared.

Boggan, it appears, either heard the conversation between Pearson and his father, or was notified by some ally of what was happening, I know not which. At any rate he slipped out of the house, fled the swamps and escaped.

Col. Cash was placed under arrest and his rifle and pistols taken away from him. This he protested against as an outrage and declared he only yielded to the force of superior numbers.

In the morning Captain Richbourg went to Cheraw and applied to the authorities for fifty men to aid him in scouring the swamps for Boggan. It was Sunday morning and everybody in Cheraw was at church (the people of Cheraw are all very pious). When the desire of Captain Richbourg was made known, there was a loud commotion in Cheraw. One poor old fellow was instantly taken with a terrible pain in his stomach while another actually vomited all over himself.

The beauty of Cheraw, however, encouraged the chivalry to "shoulder arms" and march away after bloody Boggan, and soon the Pee De swamps were being raked as with a fine-tooth comb, but no trace of the "wanted one" could be found.

The arrest of Col. Cash was on the ground of his being "accessory after the fact" of Boggan's crime. He was taken to Columbia and lodged in jail, where he was detained until Wednesday, March 12th, when he was released under the writ of habeas corpus and placed under a $3,000 bond for his appearance at the May term of the Superior court for Chesterfield county.

Owing to the sympathy which had been aroused in the poplar mind for Col. Cash after the death of his son, the Solicitor deemed it well not to give out the bill of indictment against him at the May term of said court, and the case was continued until the September session, when Col. Cash, it is supposed, will be placed upon trial as an "accessory after the fact" in the murder of W. H. H. Richards; and perhaps as "accessory before the fact." The penalty for the former offence is imprisonment in the State penitentiary; for the latter—hanging!

Let all lovers of justice unite in hoping that when Col. Cash is placed upon trial for his crime, he will receive that punishment which he so justly merits.

CHAPTER X.

The Bloody Death of Bloody Boggan Cash.

Soon after the failure of Constable Richbourg to capture Boggan Cash, Col. Cash and his minions industriously circulated the report that the murderer had fled the country. This report found a certain credence almost everywhere except in Chesterfield county. There, however, the Cashes were too well known for the people to believe any such a tale. They rightly believed Boggan Cash to be hiding in the swamps, and as the time drew nigh for holding the Court, there was a popular, if not a loud, demand for the apprehension of the outlaw. The pressue brought to bear upon him growing stronger day by day, Sheriff Spofford, in the early part of May, announced that, a certain time he would hunt for Boggan Cash. It is said he also notified Boggan of his intentions and warned him to be on the lookout, lest he be caught napping. At the appointed time about fifty men responded to his call and they set out in quest of the murderer. Unfortunately the Sheriff got drunk, lost his way, fell in a ditch and the expedition came to naught.

A few days after this disgraceful affair, Solicitor Newton ordered Sheriff Spofford to turn the papers over to his deputy, Ezekiel T. King, and that gentleman was instructed to take Boggan. Mr. King proceeded as becomes a man of sense and discretion. He picked eight men whom he knew he could trust, and then secured the services of a guide, living in the vicinity of Boggan's plantation, to lead him and his posse to the outlaw's rendezvous. Under cover of night they proceeded to the place where Boggan was supposed to be lodged. This was in a barn on Boggan's plantation, about three miles from the Cash mansion and within a hundred yards of the Pee Dee Swamp. The barn was surrounded and the approach of daylight awaited. It was understood beforehand, among the posse, that some of them, in all probability, would be killed, but they accepted the situation and not a man flinched.

Boggan was soon ascertained to be in the barn, in company with Sam Lee, one of his henchmen, a notorious desperado, who, a few years ago, under circumstances of greatest atrocity, murdered a young man while on his way to church or to Sunday school, and for which crime he was never punished.

About light Cash emerged from the barn, armed with a double-barrel gun, a repeating Winchester rifle, and a number of pistols buckled around him. He appears to have had no intimation of the presence of the Sheriff or his men and was leisurely making his way to the swamp, when he suddenly came upon one of the posse, who ordered him to surrender. His only reply was a shot from his rifle, which tore off one finger of the gentleman who hailed him. The fire was returned, and Boggan was shot in the thigh. He fell to the ground and continued to rapidly discharge his rifle, but out of the four succeeding shots which he fired, no damage was done. Mr. King ordered his men to take Cash alive, if possible, but his own conduct rendered it necessary that he be killed, and his blood, therefore, stains his own guilty hands.

Sam Lee, Boggan's pal, ran out of the barn when the firing commenced, but was shot in the leg and taken prisoner before he succeeded in doing any mischief. He was bound over to Court in the sum of $1,000, under charge of obstructing officers of the law in the discharge of their duty. Col. Cash became his bondsman and Lee was released.

Boggan was interred a little distance from the Cash mansion, and his mother's remains were exhumed from the cemetery in Cheraw—where they were placed at her own request and had rested for four years—to be placed beside the mortal remains of her erring son.

Col. Cash ordered that Mrs. Cash's grave be left open, as he intended to "put that d——d Henley in it and cover him up!" I do not know whether the grave were left open or not, in obedience to Col. Cash's instructions, but I do know that Henley is not at all uneasy about ever occupying it.

Had it not been for the Cheraw tragedy in February, and the consequent killing of Boggan Cash some three months later, Col. Cash would very likely have been nominated for Governor of South Carolina by the Greenback party. Even since these sad events, I think he has cherished the hope of becoming that party's standard bearer the present year. Recently, however, the wretched old man has come to understand that he is too heavy a weight for even that party to carry, and that there is no chance of his receiving its nomination. For this reason, I take it, he is again becoming restless, and the unusually quiet attitude which he has preserved since Boggan was killed, in giving place to one more desperate, perhaps, than ever.

It was currently reported, after Boggan was killed, that Col. Cash would avenge himself upon Mr. King, every member of the posse, and every person known to have encouraged, aided or abetted the officers in the discharge of their duty.

It now begins to look as if this prophecy is to be fulfilled. For sometime the identity of the person who conducted Sheriff King and posse to Boggan's castle was kept a secret. At last, however, the truth leaked out, and Mr. Pawley Douglass was "spotted." On the 18th of July, while plowing in his field Mr. Douglass was shot down by some unknown person. The ball struck a rib, glanced and came out, without causing death. The animal with which Mr. Douglass was plowing, ran away, and Mr. D., with the lines wrapped around his hands, was dragged a considerable distance, thus saving him from another shot and perhaps sparing his life.

A few minutes after the shooting, a colored woman, it is said, saw Col. Cash emerge from the bushes on horseback. Mr. Douglass recognized the report of the rifle as being the same as the one Sam Lee had been shooting in the neighborhood for several days. Between Col. Cash and Sam Lee, in my opinion, was there an attempt made to assassinate Pawley Douglass.

On the subject of this attempted assassination, Col. Cash, in a letter addressed to the Columbia Register, gives utterance to the following sentiments:

"'Leo,' writing from Cheraw, chrages me with having made threats against Pawley Douglass, the inhuman and ungrateful wretch who betrayed my son and aided in having him shot to death by the thugs and henchmen of the Ring. The statement of "Leo," as far as it refers to me, is a willful and malicious falsehood. I have made no threats against any one, since the murder of my son. So far from it, I have appealed to influential men in this county to use their influence to prevent any act of retaliation until the charges against me have been settled in court. So far as I am informed, the universal belief, in this part of the county fixes the shooting of Douglass upon those who murdered my son. They had an elephant on their hands, who, for a paltry sum, would have sold them as he sold his friend and benefactor. They supposed there would be no difficulty in fixing the suspicion on some one else; but, so far, they have made a most complete failure. I dislike very much to appear before the public, and my friends all urge me to be silent; and I now beg you and your readers (as this may be my last communication) to believe nothing you see in a newspaper about me. E. B. C. CASH.

The above communication I publish rather as a curiosity than anything else. The idea of Douglass being shot by the men who killed Boggan Cash is too absurd to mention. His own personal safety required that the part he played in leading Sheriff King and posse to Boggan's stronghold be kept a secret. The posse themselves had no interest in the matter. And how, pray, and to whom, could he sell the posse "for a paltry sum?" Fiddlesticks!

The failure to kill Douglass, may, for a time, check the murderous designs of Col. Cash and his "avenging angels," but that there will be attempts made upon the lives of other members of the posse, as well as upon a number of other persons not immediately concerned in the killing of Boggan Cash, is firmly believed. It is said that Col. Cash has down upon his "dead list" the names of at least twenty-five men whom he intends to have killed or crippled, and the public need not be surprised to hear of another tragedy at any moment.

For the present, my sketch must end here, as, at present, there is nothing else to tell, but—

THE END OF THE CASH FAMILY IS NOT YET.

www.ingramcontent.com/pod-product-compliance
Lightning Source LLC
Chambersburg PA
CBHW020237090426
42735CB00010B/1729